WAKE UP...
LIVE THE LIFE YOU LOVE

STORIES OF
TRANSFORMATION

Wake Up... Live the Life You Love
Stories Of Transformation

Little Seed Publishing
Laguna Beach, CA

COPYRIGHT © 2007 by Global Partnership, LLC

Pre-Press Management by New Caledonian Press
Text Design: Justin Kimbro

Cover Design and Illustrations: K-Squared Designs, LLC

Publisher intends this material for entertainment and no legal, medical or other professional advice is implied or expressed. If the purchaser cannot abide by this statement, please return the book for a full refund.

Acknowledgement is made for permission to quote copyrighted materials.

Distributed by Global Partnership, LLC
608-B Main Street
Murray, KY 42071

Library of Congress Cataloguing In Publication Data
Wake Up... Live the Life You Love: Stories Of Transformation
ISBN: 1-933063-06-8

$14.95 USA $19.95 Canada

WAKE UP... LIVE THE LIFE YOU LOVE

STORIES OF TRANSFORMATION

Other books by Steven E, and Lee Beard

Wake Up... Live the Life You Love

*Wake Up... Live the Life You Love,
Second Edition*

Wake Up... Shape Up... Live the Life You Love

Wake Up... Live the Life You Love...

Inspirational How-to Stories

In Beauty

Living on Purpose

Finding Your Life's Passion

Purpose, Passion, Abundance

Finding Personal Freedom

Seizing Your Success

Giving Gratitude

On the Enlightened Path

In Spirit

A Power Within

Finding Life's Passion

WAKE UP... LIVE THE LIFE YOU LOVE
STORIES OF TRANSFORMATION

How would you like to be in the next book with a fabulous group of best-selling authors? Another Wake Up book is coming soon!

Visit: WakeUpLive.com

We would like to provide you with a free gift to enhance this book experience.

For your free gift, please visit: WakeUpGift.com.

WAKE UP... LIVE THE LIFE YOU LOVE

STORIES OF TRANSFORMATION

TABLE OF CONTENTS

WAKE UP... LIVE THE LIFE YOU LOVE
STORIES OF TRANSFORMATION

STORIES OF TRANSFORMATION

FOREWORD

We are excited!

With the publication of this book, the *Wake Up . . . Live the Life You Love* book series approaches its 20th book with a very pleasant record of best-sellers and author achievements.

We are intensely pleased to pass this milestone in cooperation with the Learning Strategies organization. This dynamic group of mentors, guides, teachers and facilitators has an impressive history of providing vital, current, life-changing education and insights for learners around the world.

Paul R. Scheele, Pete Bissonette and their associates have much to celebrate. Those with whom they have worked have told their stories with humor, compassion and understanding. If words and intentions can lead to human transformations, then there are great changes ahead for this book's audience.

It has been our pleasure to work with Paul and Pete, along with Chris Chickering, Debra Hughes, and all the folks at Learning Strategies who have done so much to bring helpful, uplifting and life-changing stories to you, the reader.

We believe the stories in this book can be a major factor in helping you find your success in life and business. Always remember to make friends along the way and enjoy the journey!

To your success,

Steven E & Lee Beard

INTRODUCTION

Personal transformation often blossoms out of hopelessness and despair. Other times it is driven by anguish and painstaking work. Even mere serendipity can lead to amazing life changes.

In this inspiring collection of personal stories, you'll learn how others have met adversity, overcome harsh life circumstances, and created fulfilling lives of joyful bliss and abundance. Best-selling authors, healers, transformational leaders, teachers, coaches, and others share the pivotal moments of their lives that led them down new and innovative paths and rewarding journeys. See how their lessons learned can apply to your own life.

Co-authors include Paul R. Scheele, international learning expert and leader; Chunyi Lin, Spring Forest Qigong teacher and healer; Marie Diamond, Feng Shui expert and teacher of *The Secret*; Michael J. Bennett, award-winning teacher and researcher on human communication; and Al Siebert, internationally recognized expert on resiliency and the survivor personality.

Learn how these and dozens of others have triumphed over adversity and turned their lives into living works of passion and play in

Wake Up... Live the Life You Love's Stories of Transformation

WAKE UP...
LIVE THE LIFE YOU LOVE

STORIES OF TRANSFORMATION

A SINGLE THOUGHT CAN CHANGE YOUR LIFE
Paul R. Scheele

Changing one's entire life begins with no more effort than a shift in a single thought. That may sound simplistic, but it's exactly how the course of my life changed. In one critical moment you can change your life just as quickly and deliberately.

I was 19 years old and in college when a clinical hypnotist and acquaintance, Mrs. Zula Bowers, invited me to a hypnosis training seminar. Soon I was employed in her clinic, and one night Zula called and asked me to deliver a presentation on hypnosis to a church youth group. She explained a number of stage hypnosis tricks to use to improvise an interesting performance.

During the show I told a teenage boy that his foot was glued to the floor and he couldn't move it. This was basically a simple demonstration of muscle catalepsy, a test for "level one" hypnotic trance depth. Sure enough, try as he might, no matter how the rest of his body struggled, his foot was completely glued to the floor.

Now I was thinking, "Cool, this hypnosis trick worked!" but did my best to look calm and professional, as if I had done this sort of thing all my life. So, feeling confident in my ability, I tried a more difficult test for a "level two" trance. I looked at the young man and said, "You can try to tell me your name, but you can't. You've forgotten it." No matter how hard the boy struggled, he seemed completely unable to speak his own name.

At that moment, instead of thinking how powerful I was as a hypnotist, I immediately felt illuminated as if I were standing in a shaft of light from heaven. I thought, "Oh my gosh, we're doing this to ourselves *all the time*! Every day we take perfectly reasonable abilities, perfectly reasonable resources of mind, and throw them out, simply by accepting the suggestion that *I cannot.*"

Normal human capabilities vaporize—become impossible to access—when we focus the mind in a way that makes us believe they are not available. Simple trance phenomena can have a profound affect on everyone.

When I removed the suggestions and the boy could once again move his foot and speak his name, I realized I had been changed.

My mission was clear. It was not about putting people into a trance. My new mission was about *waking people from the trances* they were already accepting from themselves, their family, media, society, doctors, and schools.

What sort of trances are you living in today? What self-limiting beliefs are keeping you from pursuing your goals and dreams?

When you learn what a hypnotist knows about the workings of the human mind, you can take back the power of your own mind and prevent the loss of abundant resources.

Your natural abundant power that is the essence of who you are can perform what looks miraculous. Yet it is *no more miraculous* than the beating of your heart or the breath that you breathe whether you think about breathing or not.

By any definition, the miracle is you; not what you can do.

That presentation was the beginning of my career in hypnotism. In fact, I studied everything I could to further understand this window into the workings of the human mind. The fundamentals of consciousness became clearer and clearer. Consciousness is an endless stream. Our awareness simply shifts from wakefulness, to dreaming, to sleeping.

In a fraction of a second, it is possible to leave the awareness of now and enter a trance-like state that alters consciousness. In an instant, your mind can take you to thoughts and feelings that have nothing to do with your awareness of now. In a split second, your mind can take you to failures from the past and project images of limitation into the future. All of these thoughts are fictitious representations, false projections, simple momentary trances that we can attach to and amplify with the power of mind.

On the other hand, if you can appreciate the state for what it is and realize that you are the hypnotist of your own mind, then you can choose the life you want to create. You can wake from those temporary nightmares of imagination and find freedom in a trance-free zone, a place of consciousness and bliss that comes way before thoughts, feelings, beliefs and hypnosis.

I've seen recovery from illnesses, allergies, anxieties, and many other physical, emotional, and mental problems. I've even helped people recover from comas and brain surgery, and I've worked in dental and medical clinics helping people experience invasive work without pain, unnecessary bleeding or anxiety of any kind, and heal rapidly afterward.

Fixing problems, although interesting, was more of a laboratory to confirm my theories of human development. My years of exploring human consciousness showed me that there is more going on than can be attributed to the workings of the conscious mind. From a hypnotist's perspective, it is obvious that information is processed outside of conscious awareness. Research in cognitive psychology confirms this finding. But from the view of the conscious mind, conditioned by societal norms, the notion of nonconscious processing is mystical, at best, and easily dismissed.

Imagine what these insights gave me. It was like walking behind the curtain of the great and powerful Oz. It was like getting off of a ride at Disneyland to look behind at the electronics and mechanics that make it all work. It was like going to the magic shop and learning the trick that the stage magician used to baffle an audience.

During my hypnosis demonstration with the youth group, in one moment of revelation, I experienced a personal transformation. I gained a whole new understanding of the mind's tremendous capabilities and how to release them for the benefit of humanity. Since that time, my life's work has been clear: awaken people from their self-limiting trances so that they can reclaim the magnificence of who they really are.

What do you need to make your own personal transformation? I'll give you the complete guide to transformation in two simple sentences:

1. The words you speak out loud and silently to yourself are powerful commands to your vast nonconscious mind.
2. Eliminate the words "I can't" and direct your thinking to what you now choose to create.

Everyone can learn how to undo the trances they live under day in and day out. Once you know what is going on, it isn't magic at all. When you use the brain for positive change, results will appear far more powerful than magic.

Sharing how to use the vast talents of the brain for positive change is why I started Learning Strategies Corporation back in 1981. I wanted to create home study courses, such as *Natural Brilliance*, to help people learn about the fabulous human talents that are being squandered, thrown out, or dismissed, simply because they've never been informed about what is going on inside them.

The opportunity to awaken from trances and step into your abundance and power can occur wherever you are, now and into the future. Simply learn to consistently direct your thoughts and you can create the life you desire.

Paul R. Scheele

SURRENDER AND LIVE THE LIFE YOU WANT TO LIVE NOW
A. Alex Viefhaus

"Don't worry, tomorrow could be worse."

I wrote those words on a poster I made for my mother many years ago to help pull her out of a slump after our family business failed. "There is no point in worrying about tomorrow," I wanted to tell her. "You may as well make today happy."

It took me many years to learn my own message. It wasn't until I surrendered worrying that I learned the power of true detachment. In 2002 I had not hit rock bottom, yet, I experienced five years of personal losses that left me on a disability pension with savings that could only last until 2007. It would not be possible to survive on the pension alone. I was 40 years young, frustrated, and worried about my future.

I found a boyfriend, only to lose him within 11 months. "I'm sorry I can't handle your disability," he said. "I'm going to see if I can find another woman." Words cannot describe how much it hurt. We had started a business together, and now I was left to build it on my own. I didn't have a choice. I had to handle my disability.

Then I lost my home, so my savings were going toward rent. The pension wasn't sufficient enough to support myself and, while I hoped the business would succeed, it failed in spite of all my actions.

I was doing all the visualizations and affirmations I thought would help me create a better life, yet I could not see a future. Then, one morning I woke up and knew what my problem was. The answer came in this message: "Don't worry, tomorrow could be worse."

The problem was, I did worry that tomorrow could be worse, and I wanted to control it and make sure it wasn't. My visualizations and affirmations weren't giving me the control I wanted. I finally saw the underlying fear: I was not in control. I was afraid I wasn't doing it right. The nagging doubts multiplied. *What if it's wrong? What if I created more trouble with this affirmation? Is my visualization detailed enough? Why isn't it working yet?*

As I looked at my past, it was obvious I couldn't exert much control over my future. If I'd had control then, I wouldn't be in this mess now. I desperately wanted to control my future so I could live the life I wanted. But in attempting to do so, I missed the only time I could live the life I wanted to live: right now. This is the only moment I am alive. Everything else is just imagination.

It's impossible to control the future just as it is impossible to control the past. When I understood this, I surrendered. I quit worrying about it. I gave up being afraid of what the future might hold.

Have you ever noticed how we handle whatever comes along anyway? The sense of relief and peace that filled me the moment I let go of trying to be in control of my future brought me to the now and that's just fine.

Wanting to have control of our money, wanting someone who loves and supports us, or wanting the freedom to fulfill our desires keeps us focused on a future that might never exist. We hope the future we think we want is the one that will happen. We dream and plan because we are afraid of what will happen if we don't do something about it. We don't control it. I had financial security, owned my own house, and expected a steady income into my old age. I lost it all anyway.

My fears prevented me from living the life I wanted to live. I was cheating myself and didn't even know it. I thought I had the Law of

Attraction working for me, but it worked against me because I unwittingly focused on my worries and fears.

When I honestly look at what I am doing right now, everything is fine as it is. I am comfortable. I am at peace. I think about the wonderful experiences already in my life, and nothing in the future can guarantee that. The bills that are due later don't need attention now. Right now I'm doing something else. Why spoil this moment by worrying about something that can only be taken care of in the future? The weight of the world lifted off my shoulders when I realized this.

By surrendering, I discovered when I can live the life I want to live. The time is now—right now, not some point in the future when everything is right. It is not when we own a dream home with scenic views, a big expensive car, or have the money for overseas vacations. These things are merely what we think money will give us. We think they will bring us inner peace, love, security, and assurance that everything will always be taken care of. We wish that health problems, disabilities, and pains will disappear so we can have inner peace, love, and security. We need to relax and stop worrying about the future. I don't have to wait for the future to be free of worry. I can do that now by choosing not to worry about how I will cope in the future, and just enjoy the peace and joy I find in my life now.

By surrendering, everything started falling into place.

I studied the *PhotoReading* personal learning course from Learning Strategies Corporation and discovered how much you can learn from other people (authors) when you change how you read. I was so excited by the PhotoReading whole mind system that I traveled to the United States twice to learn more. Now I am doing what I love: I'm a certified instructor!

I'm building a teaching and coaching business I never dreamed was possible because of my disability. When I visualize my future, I surrender. It may not show up that way and that's okay, because right now everything is perfect as it is.

If I am not living the life I want to live right now, then I am too busy worrying about the future: one that may or may not become a reality. Since I am here and, technically, still physically disabled, I am already handling it all anyway. The only choice I need to make now is, "Do I want to worry about the future or be at peace now?" In choosing peace, more and more my life has unfolded in exciting ways I never imagined.

Detach, let go, surrender, and live the life you want to live now. The future can hold greater things than we can imagine, and everything we imagine about the future is just a potential experience.

A. Alex Viefhaus

I CLIMBED THE LADDER OF SUCCESS WITH WORDSMITHERY

J. Michael Bennett, Ed.D.

I've had many titles in my life: kid, sergeant, boss, Doc—just to name a few. My college students used the nickname "Dr. B." Officially, I'm Dr. J. Michael Bennett, Professor Emeritus of Rhetoric at the University of Minnesota. That's not as unique or important as it sounds; I'm just one of the many thousands of professors and other members of the clerisy in the world; but I'll take it. It sounds good, it's true, and I think I earned it.

I was 28 years old when I started college. I was a house painter and paper hanger at that time. That's one bodacious occupational change! Painting and decorating is a fine job—you spend your days making the world a more beautiful and pleasant place, and you make people happy. I liked it, and I was pretty good at it. But in my estimation, professoring is better. It's a bit like what the rough-and-ready actor John Wayne is said to have quipped: "I've been rich and I've been poor. Rich is better."

Professors usually don't get rich, of course, but teaching and researching is a wonderful way to spend your life. Helping other people be all they can be is very rewarding and fulfilling for the teacher and the learner. Being well-spoken and well-read is a huge asset toward becoming all you can be in our American society. Strong communication skills are the bedrock of any field or endeavor.

Obviously, I've taken an alternative route or two in my walk through life and, for the most part, "I've done it my way." Such a road takes longer to traverse. One gets bumped around a little and stuck in a rut or two, but "all roads lead to Rome," as they say, and my "Rome" was a tenured professorship at one of the largest and best universities in the world.

Over my 30 years of professional experience, I have been fortunate enough to reach an estimated 250,000 learners through college classes, my books and personal learning courses, and in professional communication seminars sponsored by my consulting firm, The Reading Company. It still seems surreal that I earned such an opportunity and capitalized on it.

A wonderful thinker and writer named Henry David Thoreau walked his own walk, too. In his powerful and inspiring book *Walden* he counseled the world about people like himself and me and, very likely, you. Thoreau said:

"Why should we be in such desperate haste to succeed, and in such desperate enterprises? If a person does not keep pace with his companions, perhaps it is because he hears a different drummer. Let him step to the music which he hears, however measured, or far away."

Thoreau truly was a Renaissance man who knew firsthand that our wonderful differences could be a good thing! And what a wordsmith he was. Thoreau also said, *"I should not talk so much about myself if there were anybody else whom I knew as well."*

I agree, and this piece is more about me than I usually share. I'm afraid, however, that I must stay the course until I've answered the two questions you probably have at this point: *How did you do it? How can I do it, too?*

I did it with words. I think you can, too, if you are willing to work at it.

There was work, and luck, and tenacity, and pushing the envelope, and financial help, and lots of support, of course. But the fuel that made the machine run was my deliberate acquisition of a powerful, exact, and always-expanding vocabulary.

I remember a long and inspirational conversation I had with my mother when I was 12 years old about the magical power of using just the right word. She told me about Humpty Dumpty who, shortly before his fabled fall, cheekily and peevishly told Alice that any word meant whatever he wanted it to mean! Humpty was wrong, as are those who minimize the power of wordsmithery.

Mom told of some of the world's most influential and truly powerful people, the people who did their work with words, not with guns or money; people such as Jefferson and Lincoln, Churchill and Twain, Dickinson and Shakespeare—people I wanted to be like. She shared many other things about the fabulous benefits of owning and using an extensive and excellent vocabulary. She was wonderful and she was "spot on" that rainy tropical day in Miami so long ago. I still love her for it.

That interlude with my mother is where my conscious love of reading, and the excellent vocabulary that is its product, first took root. During those younger years my mom and dad helped by spending many evenings with my sister and me in friendly word competitions. Now I'm doing the same with my kids.

Ten years passed quickly. I had entered three professions at which I had done very well, and then abandoned. I felt like a quitter, an ingrate, a bit of a vagabond. I remember wondering from time to time, in quiet moments on a boat, or in a book, or at my job, what happened to my wonderfully wide-open and promising future? I was living a decent life, but one bereft of challenge, anticipation, deep satisfaction or monetary success. I was indubitably, verily, categorically stuck! I felt lost, confused, and ashamed. What was the matter with me?

I had to change directions yet again. I had to be *somebody.*

So, I decided I needed to learn more and off I went to college. On the college placement exam, I squeaked into the third quartile on the

Quantitative section, a decent score for me—especially a decade after high school graduation.

My score on the Verbal section, however, was another matter. The counselors were astounded, and I was encouraged, by my scoring in the 99th percentile. I missed one word, misanthrope—a hater of mankind. Somehow that amuses the teacher/helper in me.

Only later did I understand why I did so well after such a long academic hiatus. I had never stopped reading widely and well, noticing the words the authors used to paint their pictures.

One academic scholarship followed another. I won a Ford Foundation Fellowship, which (with the G.I. Bill and my part-time painting income) put me through a bachelor's, a master's, and a doctoral degree. From start to finish, my "twelve-cylinder" vocabulary was the catalyst and linchpin of my advancement. I had a vocabulary that started strong and grew more powerful each year of my life. It's still growing.

I moved from painter to professor in 10 years. Not bad for an average guy armed only with a love of reading and a penchant for words. I'm sure it helps to be *a wunderkind*, but you don't have to be. You have to do the necessary work, and then some, and you must really want it (whatever "it" is), but you don't have to be a paragon of any kind.

You do, however, as my life is testament, need to read, and write, and speak, and listen as accurately and as widely as you possibly can.

Oh, yes, and mind the words. They will serve you as well as they did the person who wrote or spoke them. Be all you can be.

J. Michael Bennett, Ed.D.

Feng Shui Changed My Life... Overnight
Marie Diamond

When I was 15 years old, I was run over by a truck. That was the culminating event of many tumultuous years, and it led to an experience that transformed my life forever.

I had a lot of problems in my young life. I grew up Catholic in Belgium and was very religious. I was a top student and loved to read religious books. My fellow students thought I was "nerdy." They bullied me at school and teased me about becoming a nun. They beat me up several times because they said I was "too good," or "too close" to the teachers. I had no friends because anyone who tried to be my friend at school was bullied as well. I also had several accidents and spent a lot of time at home.

One day, as I was biking home for lunch, an enormous truck pulling two large containers came speeding along. The driver didn't see me. In the curve of the road, he pulled his truck too close and struck me. I was thrown 150 feet ahead, with my face sliding against the gravel stones for more than 30 feet, completely disfiguring my face. The accident left me in a coma, and at one point they thought they had lost me. But I came back to the living.

When I was at home recuperating, I began to pray from morning until evening. I prayed all day, forgiving my enemies and all of the people who had bullied me. I asked my spiritual master, "What did I do wrong? I am a good girl. There is no girl more Catholic than me at school. What did I do wrong?" Suddenly I received an insight, a message telling me I had bad Feng Shui.

Of course, I had never heard of this before. I learned Feng Shui is an ancient Chinese art and science based on laws that govern the flow of energy. This universal energy continuously flows in and around our homes and workplaces from all directions of the compass, and it is possible to live in the energy in "wrong" ways that deplete our own energy. By following certain principles (knowing which directions are beneficial and which are not) we can actually enhance the impact of energy on our lives.

I discovered I was sleeping in the wrong room, toward the wrong direction. I immediately and instinctively understood how I could be in the wrong room. My bedroom was on the second floor of our house and directly below was the family room. My parents and siblings were always fighting in that room.

I moved to a room in the west end of the house and switched my bed so I slept toward a new direction. I painted the room orange and the furniture white.

I also became inspired to create my own art. I painted happy things and things to inspire me. I was creating my own reality with these paintings of things I really wanted to have. I wanted to have friends. I wanted to have fun and romance. I was fifteen, looking for my first love. I wanted to be a success.

I didn't completely understand it at the time, but I was creating good Feng Shui!

The orange and white colors turned out to be particularly good for me, because, as I eventually learned, they activated earth and metal energies that supported me. The room, the bed and the desk all turned out to be excellent sources of energy.

It was incredible. I became so happy just by painting the walls and the furniture.

My old room had been on the north side of our house and was painted blue with striped wallpaper. The direction and colors had been depleting my energy. I had hated that room, but since my parents had given it to me, I had always accepted it. As I looked back on it, I saw that the corner of the room that represented my "success" had a large wooden cabinet full of junk. In my "relationship" corner there was a sink that was surely sinking all of my relationships. There was no good energy there for me at all. Just moving to the new room with new colors and new directions brightened up my life. I felt a difference almost immediately.

If you surround yourself with a new environment and colors, you, too, can change your whole life. Soon I was joyfully going to school with a completely different energy. I had opened my life with the color orange—the color of celebration—and white—the color of purity.

The students who had bullied me stopped, and situations arose where I was even able to help them in such a way that they could see I was not a nasty person. Within a month they became my friends. Suddenly, I was popular. I had a group of friends, even a best friend, and I was invited to parties. It was amazing. My life was changing.

Right away I met a boy and it was love at first sight. He was "Mr. Popular," and I was "Miss Unpopular." He started waiting for me after school and, all of a sudden, people were noticing that this cute guy with a red motorcycle was with me. My popularity soared and everybody wanted to be my friend!

The Feng Shui changes I made in my room positively affected my family as well. The new colors in the west end of our home improved the relationship between my parents. The orange I painted provided much-needed earth energy. Also, the relationship between my parents and siblings improved and more people began to visit our home.

I was not aware of all of this consciously but I saw what was happening.

I remember wanting to know more about it, but in 1978, I could find no explanations of Feng Shui in Dutch. However, I knew at some point I would receive another message when it was time.

In the meantime, I made sure every house or apartment I lived in was in a westerly direction, and I always painted with the colors orange and white. The few things I knew with certainty I kept using, and they kept working. I always had good friends and wonderful people around me.

I went on to study law and become an attorney, but when I was 31, the first book on Feng Shui in Dutch was released and I knew I was studying the wrong law. I began to study the Universal Laws of Energy and with the world's greatest Feng Shui masters, becoming a Feng Shui master myself. I have a rare gift: I can see auras around people and energy flowing within rooms, much like water flowing in a river. I can see how colors, objects, and shapes affect energy and how the flow of energy in a room affects the energy of a person.

I wanted to demystify Feng Shui and help others understand how this universal energy responded to them personally, so I created my personal learning course called Diamond Feng Shui with Learning Strategies Corporation. Today I travel the world, dedicating my life to helping others use this magnificent power to create balance, harmony, and good fortune in their lives.

With the energy of Feng Shui, you too can change your life—even overnight!

Marie Diamond

Stranger Than Fiction: How Questions Awakened and Freed My Mind
Al Siebert, Ph.D.

Science fiction books were always my favorite reading. I'd lose myself in stories about a pleasant, ordinary man or woman suddenly forced into survival struggles caused by deceptive, hidden enemies. I was fascinated by characters whose efforts to survive drew out abilities and strengths they didn't know they had. The story of Neo in The Matrix is a good recent example.

Never in my own fantasies did I imagine that a similar experience might be awaiting me.

My personal journey, the adventure that awakened me and transformed me, took place in the world of hospital psychiatry and clinical psychology. But my story has broader implications: It is about learning how to think for yourself instead of believing what you are trained to think. It's about freeing your mind from social illusions and discovering truths about the world that no one tells you. It's about not allowing other people to define who you are.

My transforming adventure began as I was completing my doctoral program in clinical psychology at the University of Michigan in 1965. Something didn't seem right. "Why do I keep hearing that I'm in the mental health field?" I wondered. "I've never had a course or even one lecture on what it is like to be mentally healthy." The total focus in my clinical program was on the diagnosis and treatment of mental illnesses.

During staff meetings at the university hospital's psychiatric institute, where I worked as a psychologist, I wondered, "Why are people who think and talk in ways that upset psychiatrists declared 'schizophrenic' when no one knows what schizophrenia is, what causes it, or how to cure it? Why don't psychiatrists question their assumptions? Why are most psychiatrists incompetent, yet allowed to blame their patients when their treatments don't work? Is it possible that the perception of mental illness in a patient is actually a stress reaction in the mind of the doctor?"

An opportunity to test my hypothesis immediately presented itself. A young woman was admitted to the psychiatric institute and diagnosed as a paranoid schizophrenic. A senior psychiatrist said she was so severely mentally ill she'd probably spend the rest of her life in a state hospital on a back ward. He told the staff to start the paperwork to transfer her.

I arranged to conduct an experimental interview with her before she was transferred. During my interview, I did not allow my mind to have any thoughts of mental illness about her. Instead, I talked with her as an understanding friend and explored with her the relationship between her feelings and what was happening in her mind. Soon after, she had what a senior psychiatrist called a "spontaneous remission"—an instance when a patient suddenly recovers and the doctors don't know why. The plans to commit her were dropped, and she was transferred to the open ward and readied for discharge.

Once it began, the synchronicity between my questions and meaningful incidents continued week after week. Exciting new insights kept coming and coming. I realized that people designated as good nouns, such as "doctors," must surround themselves with bad nouns, such as "schizophrenics," to provide a contrasting frame of reference for their good noun. It's a child's personality theory acted out by many adults, but good nouns can never succeed at curing, saving, or destroying bad nouns because they need bad nouns as a basis for their esteemed identity.

I left Michigan and moved to Topeka, Kansas, to start a two-year postdoctoral fellowship in clinical psychology at the famous Menninger psychiatric clinic. The fellowship was a significant honor. Out of dozens of applicants from all over the world, I was one of only three who were selected.

When my supervisor and a psychiatrist at Menninger's asked me to tell them what I thought, I explained to them my hypothesis that the perception of mental illness in a patient is mostly a stress reaction in the minds of the doctors. I told them about my experimental interview with the young woman and how her so-called schizophrenia immediately disappeared.

Their reaction proved that my hypothesis was correct. They declared me severely mentally ill, cancelled my fellowship, and insisted that I needed years of treatment in a mental hospital.

I felt like a character in a science fiction story, except that this was stranger than any fiction I'd read. My reaction was one of surprise and fascination. I decided to allow myself to fully experience a postdoctoral education far more revealing about how psychiatry really works than what I would have learned in two years of seminars. I was fascinated as I watched leading mental health professionals react with anxiety to my ideas instead of listening with understanding. I was amazed to see these experts could not tell the difference between a transforming breakthrough and an emotional breakdown.

Understanding their distress, I was patient with them. I tried for a month to help them see how their lack of self-insight kept them trapped in a dysfunctional system, but I finally gave up. They never accepted that I define who I am, that there was nothing "sick" about me for not letting them define who I am.

As I drove out of Topeka, a powerful feeling came flooding up in me. For the first time in my life my mind was free. Until that moment, I had never suspected that my mind had been controlled by invisible constraints, that my perceptions and beliefs had been distorted by false realities I had obediently learned in my courses. I felt elated. I shouted over and over, "My mind is free!"

My marvelous Menninger adventure was the best experience of my life. Awakening from a dream world of social illusions and constructed realities gave me a significant advantage in my new professional life. I used my research skills to study the inner nature of life's most resilient survivors—people who are outstanding examples of excellent mental health.

The basis for my effectiveness as an author, teacher and speaker is simply that I describe successful patterns of actions, feelings, and thoughts that anyone can learn by asking and answering questions.

My own questions allowed my complex inner nature to emerge. I found that my adaptability, personal freedom, and effectiveness increased as I accepted counterbalanced traits into my conscious identity. I enjoyed discovering that I'm a cooperative nonconformist, a sort of responsible rebel with pessimistic optimism, sensitive toughness, selfish unselfishness, indifferent compassion, playful seriousness and more.

My awakening experience taught me how to handle the transforming process from inside the action. I've converted many difficulties into personal growth by learning valuable lessons in the school of life. You can, too.

Through my work as Director of the Resiliency Center and in my personal learning course published by Learning Strategies Corporation called *Resiliency: The Power to Bounce Back*, I help others learn to conduct their own personal transformation. Here are the steps to get you started:

1. Express your feelings; then describe what happened.

2. Ask yourself: Why is it good that this happened? What can I learn from this? What might I do differently next time?

3. Imagine yourself getting a better outcome the next time that this, or something similar, occurs.

4. Look forward to the next opportunity to use your new skill.

This works. You can do it. Just ask.

Al Siebert, Ph.D.

I Was Born a Healer...and So Were You
Chunyi Lin

A healer in every family and a world without pain—that is my life's mission.

When people first hear this, they often laugh or shake their heads in disbelief. They probably think, "This man must be crazy!"

But once they know what I know, once they see how truly simple it is to help themselves heal—and to help other people heal themselves—through the practice of Qigong, their doubt soon turns to amazement, then joy.

I understand their skepticism. Having grown up in China, I was aware of the ancient practice of Qigong, but I never truly understood its full power until years later when, as an adult, I was completely healed of the excruciating pain that had left me barely able to walk.

Qi (pronounced chee) means "energy" and gong means "to practice or refine." We are all born with this vital and intelligent life force and have the ability to balance and cultivate it through meditation and movement. However, during China's Cultural Revolution anyone would have been arrested for openly practicing Qigong.

Our family was considered "suspect" by the Communist factions, and my childhood became terrifying when my parents, simple mineworkers, were arrested because they were good people.

My three siblings and I were driven out of our home in the wintertime and forced to live in the streets because no one dared take us in. For days we lived in fear, with no food, as bullets and bombs exploded near our hiding places. Eventually someone took us in. Later, friends helped us escape to our grandmother's home until it was safe to return to our parents once again.

It was a dreadful existence. Other children insulted and hurt us. My uncle, a farmer, was tortured and killed. We lived in constant fear. We lived in hell. As time passed, I became angry and depressed.

In high school, I met a Qigong master who agreed to teach me in secret. Whenever I felt miserable, the meditations and movements he taught helped me feel better.

After high school, I was forced to work as a farmer and laborer, and I suffered still more injuries. But I continued to learn about traditional Chinese medicine. When the Cultural Revolution ended, I went on to college and began to teach English. I also continued to play basketball—a sport I loved.

Unfortunately, one day as I was moving in for a lay-up during a game, a player ran into me and I had to twist my body to avoid landing on him. Instead, I landed awkwardly on my right foot. My right knee cracked. My forward momentum carried me further, and I next landed on my left foot. My left knee cracked. I crashed to the floor in pain and had to be carried out. The cartilage damage to both knees was extensive, and surgery could not guarantee results. Arthritis developed, and the swelling and pain only got worse. I could hardly sleep, and my legs often failed me.

Then one day I (and 15,000 other people) entered a soccer stadium to attend a workshop offered by a powerful Qigong master. For over seven hours I listened with closed eyes and experienced sensations of every kind throughout my body as the Qigong master passed energy to us. Long forgotten love, kindness, compassion and forgiveness came flooding back to me.

When the workshop ended that evening, I stood up. A miracle had happened! My knee pain was almost gone. I ran and jumped about the soccer field just like a kid. I was so happy!

I continued to practice what the Qigong master taught us that day, and the remaining pain in my knees soon disappeared, never to return. I was not only physically healed, but the depression, anger and emotional pain I had felt for so many years were gone as well. I realized that our world is so beautiful.

I had experienced the healing power of Qigong; I knew I wanted to make it part of my life and help heal others. For years I studied with the greatest masters and, to my surprise, was certified as an International Qigong Master. Most of the teachings were secretive and very complicated, and most masters demanded between 15 and 50 years of practice before you were allowed to heal others.

While I greatly respected all of my masters, this never seemed right to me. From the very beginning of my Qigong training, a voice kept telling me, "Qigong is so simple. Anyone can do it. Everyone can do it."

I decided I would use my knowledge to create a new style of Qigong so simple anyone could learn it, and I called it *Spring Forest Qigong*.

You may think Qigong is something mysterious or magical or supernatural. Albert Einstein said, "The most beautiful thing we can experience is the mysterious. It is the source of all true art and science." It is the mystery that leads us to wonder and to search, discover and learn. Once the discovery is made and you reach understanding, then the initial mystery is gone.

Spring Forest Qigong is like this. It seems mysterious, but once you understand it, you realize it's not mysterious at all.

You might be surprised to learn that you've been practicing a type of Qigong since you were born—sleeping.

Sleeping is a natural meditation; it is one way our bodies balance our energy. It's a passive way of practicing Qigong. By actively practicing Qigong, you can awaken your healing energy to help you heal physically as well as mentally, emotionally, and spiritually.

Scientists have long recognized that everything in the universe, what we see and even what we cannot see, is composed of dynamic energy. You are an energy being. As Einstein proved, energy can neither be created nor destroyed—but energy can be transformed, changed, and put to use.

When you heat water, it becomes steam. The energy of the water still exists but just in a different form. It is the same with Qigong. You work with the energy, transform it, and put it to use. Illness is a form of energy you can transform into something beautiful.

No words can reveal the joy and happiness in my heart when people walk out of my office without their pain. Since I arrived to America, I have taught tens of thousands of people how to use Qigong through my classes, retreats, and my *Spring Forest Qigong* personal learning course published by Learning Strategies Corporation. These people have learned the beautiful gift of energy healing, and they are joyfully helping me achieve my mission to have *a healer in every family and a world without pain.*

When the initially skeptical ask, as they so often do, if I was born a healer, I just smile and nod. Yes, I was born a healer, and so were you!

Chunyi Lin

DON'T WAIT FOR THE PIANO TO DROP ON YOU
Nina Potter

It's been said that if God taps you on the shoulder and you don't answer, he drops a piano on you. Don't wait for the piano. Life is just *so* good when you open the door to your heart and answer your calling. I know this to be absolutely true.

I started waking up 18 long, slow years ago. My business had failed, my husband had left me, and I was driving cross-country with my best friend; all that I possessed was in the car with me. I had cried for two weeks in an ocean of self-pity before I realized that the television had not been on since he had left, I was only 30 years old, and I had my life back. I had a clean start. I didn't have much more to lose—no job, savings, spouse, kids, home, furniture—just a pile of debt. And yet, I had *so much*!

I had a friend who was willing to leave her young family to come out and rescue me. I had a loving family back home that willingly welcomed me into their home even though there was no room. (They shared their closets and beds with me!) I had my health and my education and, more than that, I had my attitude of gratitude and was free to recreate my entire life. What a gift!

I was waking up from a lifelong sleep of unconscious living. I had to start from scratch. What a challenge it was to find freedom a double-edged sword as I wrestled with restlessness, paced with indecision, and paused with self-doubt at every new opportunity. My brother reminded me, "If you're on the wrong road, it doesn't do any good to speed." So I slowed down my urgent striving and listened to my heart.

That's when I began my 12-year search for passion and purpose. I began a love affair with personal development that has blossomed into a transformation I never could have dreamed of. It has taken many years of learning, practicing, seeking and questioning to find the daily practices that would feed my soul and open my heart.

After experimenting with more than five careers, I finally discovered that the thing I love to do more than anything else in the world is coach. *Coach*? I was already doing it with everyone I connected with who was going through a divorce or career change. For some reason I was a magnet for anyone experiencing a major life change. The only problem was that, at the time, there wasn't a career path for coaching. I didn't recognize that this was an opportunity to develop something new. I saw only that I would need 6 to 8 more years of college to become a psychologist. I didn't even want to be a psychologist!

I did the next best thing. I put my heart into my current career and found all the ways to do what I love within that work. It was satisfying by day but I kept having that nagging sensation that there had to be more. There had to be a way to live the full expression of who I am and live the life of my dreams. I kept having that thought and trusting that I would find it one day. I prepared for the time when I could make the transition, whatever and whenever that would be.

When it happened, I was ready. I had just been laid off from a job I had only taken to save me from the former job that was killing me. I was determined never again to work a job that didn't fulfill my purpose and passion in life. I heard about an emerging field called "coaching" and I knew it was exactly what I was looking for. I began training and started a small practice. I loved the work—it wasn't even work; it was fun. Yet, something was still missing.

I realized that I had been asking the wrong questions. I finally stopped and asked myself, "What will I be experiencing when I'm finally living my perfectly intended life?" I discovered, to my amazement, that the one thing that would matter more than anything else in the world would be to live my life feeling fully connected to God. To me, God is the all, the everything, in me, in you, in everyone, in perfection just as it is. I had not attended more than 10 religious services since my childhood, so you can imagine how surprised I was to discover this from that simple question.

Since that discovery, I have had the experience of absolute connection to all, and everything was directly revealed to me in a profound and life-altering way. I have finally tasted the joy and peace that, before, were only words to me. I may not live in that experience from moment to moment, but I now know what is true, real, and possible. My life is now completely worth living. Every day is now a new opportunity to discover, to grow, to practice, and to be. The scales are falling away from my eyes and revealing the beautiful possibility of a life lived in love instead of fear.

I no longer feel those old, dreaded bouts of hopelessness or helplessness or worthlessness that used to sneak up on me and steal my desire to live. I now live in a place of deep inspiration rather than trumped up external motivations. My relationships with friends and family are easier and more intimate. My clients are joyfully finding truer meaning and purpose for the first time in their lives. My career is blossoming. It's a wonderful feeling to realize that, not only do you win when you live your life with intention, but that everyone around you wins as well.

This is the power of living your life with the intention of your heart's deepest desire. It doesn't matter what it is, only that you live it. If you don't yet know what your desire is, start living from whatever comes from the question, "What will I be experiencing when I'm finally living my perfectly intended life?" Those answers will lead you forward until you find it. Start living for your deepest desire and begin loving your life now!

Nina Potter

A Voice for All Creatures
Elizabeth Severino, M.B.A., D.D., D.R.S.

Imagine, as a young child, you're living on a farm of many acres, walking through dense woods and hearing trees speak, understanding the wood-land creatures, seeing in your mind's eye what they are seeing and feeling what they are feeling. It's the early 1950's and there are fields of horses, cows, other farm animals, and companion animals including dogs and cats in this beautiful Chester Springs, Pennsylvania setting. And you can understand them all.

Envision walking beside you is your uncle, who has the gift of healing through laying-on-of-hands and a deep love for and connection with animals. He shares with you the magnificent impressions and sounds of the *Song of Creation*. A guide to you in your early youth, he helps you realize both of you share the gift of speaking with and hearing easily the communications from all of nature; feeling and knowing the origins of others' pain; feeling the deep pull to ease suffering; knowing where to place healing hands; and knowing how to send compassionate peace to another. Your child-self doesn't know yet that others don't have these same gifts, yet you are deeply imprinted.

Your life unfolds. You leave the farm for schooling. You feel different from the other children in your grade at the Baldwin School in Bryn Mawr, Pennsylvania. You hide your gifts. A new gift for learning natural languages unfolds. Your school work is extraordinary. You earn a full scholarship to Vassar College.

As a Dean's list student at Vassar, you concentrate on languages and psychology. By graduation you know English, French, German, Latin, Greek, Middle-English and some Russian. International Business Machines Corporation (IBM) hires you to work in an advanced development laboratory creating "human-oriented" computer languages. You write IBM-confidential technical journals which are very well received and begin presenting your work at technical conferences. You earn your first of a series of awards from IBM and also earn your first masters degree in computer science.

Now you leave IBM. You write your first book, *Guide to International Computer Systems Architecture*, and find yourself on the international map of computer consultants almost overnight. You're traveling the world. You marry and have a child and go back to IBM after an extraordinary offer and earn your second Master's degree, in business administration. Yet again, you leave IBM to become Vice President for McGraw-Hill/Datapro, and begin traveling the world again. Your accomplishments are chronicled in dozens of *Who's Who* books nationally and internationally including *International Leaders in Achievement* published in Cambridge, England. But now you're starting to feel that something is missing: Spirituality, connection to nature, the deep desire of the heart to be of service to animals and their people in a communicative and healing capacity and the imprint left on your being as a young child begins to call—except you don't fully listen, just yet.

A few years pass. It's now the late 1980s and you've just had a near-death experience. A myriad of natural and spiritual healing modalities allow you to heal in innumerable miraculous and magical ways. You find yourself disquieted with standard, conventional healing methods. You research and write a second book, *Do-It-Yourself Vibrant Health*; and then a third book, *Reiki: The Healer's Touch*; and a fourth book, *Diet to Raise Your Spiritual Level*. You leave the corporate world.

Around this time, a most magnificent being and friend in the body costume of a cocker spaniel comes into your life. Tanuka is your guide to the mystic healing realms, a profound teacher shining forth as your co-facilitator of workshops in spirituality, intuition, and animal communication. Your reputation as a spiritual healer, an intuitive, and an animal communicator spreads. You become a guest on radio talk shows and appear on TV to perform in healing touch for dogs and animal communication. You teach ways to raise the spiritual level and connection to all that is. You are profiled nationally for the first time in a major magazine. You meet Dr. Caroline Myss and her healing colleague, Dr. Ron Roth, and launch, enthusiastically, into their programs. You earn a doctorate in religious studies with a concentration in healing through prayer and touch. You become ordained as a spiritual healer. You find yourself specializing in veterinary medical intuition by helping animals, their humans, and their veterinarians, especially giving assistance to animals who are suffering, very old, infirm and nearing the end of their lives. The animals choose you to write their feelings about this time for them, and you write the highly acclaimed book, *The Animals' Viewpoint on Dying, Death and Euthanasia.*

You're on radio and TV, again sharing the animals' voices. You become the featured Animal Communicator in the 22-year-old highly esteemed journal, *Species Link: The Journal of Interspecies Telepathic Communication.* You appear on national TV as an animal communicator on *The Voice.* The American Holistic Veterinary Medical Association invites you to speak on "Improving Practical Intuition" at its 2006 annual convention. Your session is one of the best attended. You continue to help people and animals by voicing and sensing animals through private consultations and continue to offer workshops teaching people to open up to the "Language of Intuition" and ways to raise one's spiritual level.

You have been so blessed by grace and so disciplined by special training that the sacred energy of healing compassion flows from your very being and touches both people and animals, whose lives become better. Each animal voiced visibly demonstrates its relaxation at having been understood.

Imagine that you have become a mystic, enjoying a relationship with the "Sacred Universe" which embraces, yet also transcends, religion.

The Sacred Universe is constantly showing you its pleasure spontaneously with events and situations that create delight for you, a feeling of being very recognized and very visible to the exquisite world of Sacred Spirit. Imagine that you feel this connection deepen every day.

This is what it's like to live my life.

A prayer rendered, a prayer heard:

Sacred Universe, Most Wondrous and Most Praiseworthy,
You Make Me an Instrument of Thy Peace.
You Make it so
That I am a Voice for All Creatures
And a Healer for Those Seeking Healing.
You Make it so
That This Life's expression
Unfolds with Conscious Awareness,
Compassion, Love, Mercy, and Joy.
You Make it so
That You are in Me and I am in You
And That Together We Combine as One.
You Make it so
That the world is better for this.
And it is so.

☉ *Elizabeth Severino, M.B.A., D.D., D.R.S.*

COOK UP A NEW YOU!
Marilyn Schoeman Dow

What if, just as an experiment, you explore the re-invention of yourself? Create yourself anew by savoring and celebrating all the wondrous elements you've grown within yourself over the years. Consider what you might like to add, tweak or omit. You may discover you allowed things into your life that, upon examination, you decide you don't want anymore. Maybe you never wanted it; you didn't think about it, you just let it become a piece of yourself.

How do you choose which elements to keep in the re-created you and which ones to leave out? One option is to weigh them on the Green Light/Red Light scale. In general, Green Light® indicates the good things. Red Light indicates the other things. Just as you would use the best ingredients to bake a cake, you want to use some of your favorite personal ingredients, like passion, compassion, creativity, sense of humor and your ability to successfully complete significant projects, to create a new you. You might also sprinkle in your strengths, interests, achievements, relationships, goals, dreams and aspirations — those hearty elements that renew your self. These are Green Light® ingredients.

What color is your style? How do you think, speak, feel and act?

Red Light
What you don't like
Focus: Obstacle
Attention: OFF goal
Intention: MISS goal

Green Light®
What you prefer
Focus: Objective
Attention: ON goal
Intention: GET GOAL

Old insults, grudges, arguments, embarrassments, failures and feuds don't make it to the pot of possibilities when cookin' up the new you. Sarcasm, putdowns, belligerence, dishonesty, selfishness and cruelty belong in the garbage can. They may appear in pity party recipes (with more pity than party.) These are Red Light ingredients.

Green Light: Life is a bowl of cherries.
Red Light: Life is a pile of pits.

We can't change our history but we can change our view of it. We can't give ourselves new parents or a new childhood, but we can give ourselves a new start by picking new viewpoints. These viewpoints can range from deep, dark Red, to bright, glowing Green. It's a bit Red to expect to be Green all the time — yet it's a good target. Practice the skill of Green Light and watch your life get Greener.

Count your blessings. Red Light — I don't have ONE!
Green Light —101,102,103...

What color do you focus on?

Red Light	Green Light
*Magnify the bad stuff.**	*Magnify the good stuff.**
*Minify the good stuff.**	*Minify the bad stuff.**
What you don't have	What you have
What you don't want	What you want
What you want less of	What you want more of
What makes you scowl	What makes you smile
What makes you angry	What makes you excited
make it Red.	
*Constructive action could make it Green.	*Destructive action could make it Red.

Create a Green Light life that emphasizes positive aspects. Consider it a game: How Green can you be? How quickly can you catch yourself when you tilt toward the Red? How fast can you shift back to Green? How long can you maintain the shift? Just playing around with these questions lightens your spirit and makes it easier to make your viewpoint more positive.

Take the Green Light game a step further and view a situation as a stage production. Your life is the play. The current scene is being written. What role do you want to play? What role do you not want to play? How will you choose to play it in various situations, with various characters? Pick a scene from your recent past that didn't go the way you wanted, where you didn't handle it the way you prefer. Replay it in your mind. Rewrite the script in the way you prefer, then Green up your role in the next performance.

Who is your Chief Life Officer, your CLO? You are!

Red Light: Why I can't...
Green Light: How I can...

When you view life as a game, you can step back a bit and you see the things you missed when the focus was on how others disappointed, ignored or treated you unfairly.

To keep the game going in your favor, when you find yourself in a challenging situation, ask yourself three questions:

1. How does it look from a Green Light viewpoint?
2. How does it look from a Red Light viewpoint?
3. How do I want to see it?

Then decide to see the view you choose. Make a conscious choice instead of auto-piloting through life. That frees you from being locked in old patterns and beliefs — and seeing Red.

Green Light unlocks creativity.
Red Light blocks creativity.

When you feel yourself slipping back into Red Light modes, commend yourself for noticing, then just repeat the process: Ask the questions, choose the view. You'll soon recognize the Red earlier in the game and shift more quickly and easily.

Handle the Red stuff Greenly.

Who makes you grin? Who makes you frown? Who turns your world quite upside down? Who decides it's ease or it's strife? Who's in charge of you and your life?

Green Light - first aid for the Red, cross.

Be careful not to harp at yourself — it's not a pretty sound. Notice your self-talk. What do you whisper softly in your head? That's the Red Light stuff — discouragement, ridicule, failure feelings — a nagging, a doubting of your abilities. Switch it to Green. Talk about your successes and the goals you are working on.

Pitch those contaminated ingredients into the Red refuse bin and mine your experiences for the golden nuggets you can grasp. Keep the lessons. Lose the lectures.

Put on your Green glasses.

Who decides?
Who decides what you think, what you feel? Who decides what you say, what you do? Who decides how you view a memory? Who decides how you interpret a life event?

See the world you want.
Happiness doesn't depend on circumstances. They change.
Happiness depends on our decisions. We, too, can always change.

The most intelligent life — on any planet — is Green! So go ahead. Get the Red out. Turn yourself into a bright Green bein'! The Jolly Green Giant pales next to you!

> **Green Light: The universe is conspiring to do me good.**
> **Red Light: The universe is conspiring to do me harm.**

So WAKE UP! Live the life you love. Choose today to create a Green Light being. It's as easy as that — and as challenging. Collect the choicest Green ingredients and cook up a delicious new you — a human being Green. A Green being. 'Tis always the season for reNEWal. So grow your Greens!

Marilyn Schoeman Dow

Waiting To Live Is A Life Lived Waiting
Acey Gaspard

You have to stop before you can get started in a new direction. Well, I was stopped at a red light on Malden road in Windsor, Ontario, Canada. While I waited for the light to change, I noticed the condition of my van and decided I'd really like to get it detailed. "I'll do this once I complete my latest website," I thought. It was an old habit; accomplish a goal, then reward yourself. Many people believe as I did—withhold a desire to drive yourself toward achievement.

It occurred to me a few minutes later, "Why do I have to wait to achieve my goal in order to detail my van? I have the money, it doesn't take time out of my schedule, and I can just drop it off and pick it up the next day. What a ridiculous thought: waiting until I accomplish a goal so that I can get my van detailed."

The more I thought about it the deeper the thoughts became and then I realized it wasn't just the issue of my van. I do this often. In fact, I have been doing this most of my life. I have been putting off living and, instead, waited for better times. I would think, "When I increase my level of income I'll take more time off;" "When I'm successful in my online business, then I'll travel;" "When we have a bigger house, then I can decorate it the way I want." I recalled the many different times when I had accomplished goals and discovered I did the same thing—look towards better times rather than celebrate success. The list of these examples goes on and on and the end result is: **Waiting to live.**

About a week later, I stopped for gas at a station in Michigan. It was a regular day, there was no change in my life, I didn't achieve any goals that day, I didn't increase my income, I didn't win a lottery—nothing out of the ordinary. As I was pumping gas, I began thinking about my discovery about myself—waiting to live—and I thought to myself, "*I don't have to wait to live!* There is nothing that says that I have to wait to live. Why am I waiting for events and better times to take place so that I can start living? *I can live now*, no matter what the situation is."

At that very moment I felt a burst of energy in my chest as though a rock had been removed. I was no longer going to wait to live my life! Life is here now and I intend to live now—this minute. It was as though I had been living in a prison cell all my life. I could see the outside world through a tiny window but I couldn't get there. Now the gatekeeper opened the door and said, "Go, you are free to start living your life, starting now." I looked into the gatekeeper's face and it was my own face into which I gazed.

That was an awakening that I'll never forget. My eyes were opened and I had an abrupt change in the way I looked at life.

Now, I find myself more appreciative of what I already have in my life and I enjoy it the way it is. No more waiting for what might be. I don't feel rushed to achieve as before. This doesn't mean I have stopped setting and moving toward goals. Now I move forward with awareness. I enjoy the journey as well as arriving at the destination.

I realize it's important to live in the moment and experience all that life has to offer. Once the moment is gone, it's gone forever. If you experience life as it is, you can savor your memories. If you wait for a certain event to happen in order to start living, then all you'll have are memories of waiting to live.

What happens if you keep waiting to live? You could spend your whole life waiting for the perfect moment and better times. What if they don't arrive? For example, if you're eagerly waiting for a promotion at work, anytime something good happens to you during work, you may brush it off because it's not the promotion you've been waiting for, so there is nothing to celebrate. Let's say you never get the promotion. Then what? You didn't experience the good times that are gone forever because you were waiting. Don't wait; live life as it is, experience what life has to offer each day just the way it is, and when and if the promotion takes place, you'll enjoy it and appreciate it even more.

What can you do to start living today? You can make the decision that you will no longer wait to live your life. You can decide to start living and experience what life has to offer today. Let go of feelings of eagerness, stress and shortcoming. Experience today as it is. You don't need to have an experience as I did. All it takes is for you to identify a simple behavior. The next time you catch yourself putting off anything that brings you pleasure, pause and say to yourself, "Life is here now! There is no waiting; there is no better time to live."

God has given us the gift of life so we can experience and enjoy all this day has to offer. Start living today!

Acey Gaspard

TRANSFORMATION: ART OR SCIENCE?
Lee Beard

As I talk with people around the world, everyone wants to know the "silver bullet" to success, the "secret to happiness" and the "one key to wealth." From what I have observed, a successful life and business must have a solid spiritual foundation. After that, success seems to involve a constant transformation that becomes more of an art form than an exact science.

As I have had the opportunity to be involved in several entertainment and recreation industries, I have developed a motto that says, "To be successful in any venture, one must learn enough to ask the right questions and do enough to understand the answer."

While preparing for a conference call with Bill Bartmann, who was reported to be the 25th richest man in the U.S., I came up with a thought that seemed to describe business success in a way most people seem to understand, especially if they have had the experience of learning to drive an automobile with a manual transmission.

I remember some of my experiences when I first learned to drive. You start the car, put it in neutral, push down on the clutch, give it some gas and then let out on the clutch. During your first few attempts, the car is jerked and the motor is killed several times. Then there is popping of the clutch and banging on the steering wheel.

Once you get everything going in one direction, it's time to shift into second gear. Shifting into second gear is much like what I call "getting over the hump" in business; the point at which you are generating enough income to have a staff and do not have to do everything yourself. You put a system in place, operate by policy, and design more and more so everyone on the team can work in concert.

Finally, you get the car rolling, you let off of the gas and you have to press down on the clutch to shift to second gear. Usually there is some spitting and sputtering of the motor and grinding of the gears along with swerving in the road until you steady your hands. Then, you must master third gear, which involves more speed and other vehicles and objects to avoid along the road as your teacher hides behind the newspaper so as to avoid being scared to death by your "learning."

Now that I have written this, I realize that learning to drive a car with a manual transmission feels exactly like starting and growing a business. There will probably be a sputtering of the engine, grinding of the gears, killing of the motor and some banging on the steering wheel along the way.

Then living your life and growing your business really gets to be fun—just like driving a sports car. You don't think as much about the mechanics of the car when you are enjoying the drive and the road ahead. Your sports car and your business can take you on enjoyable trips to places you never dreamed of before. The best part of all is getting to take your friends and loved ones along for the wonderful ride.

There is a scientific way to drive and shift a car if you watch your tachometer, but always driving and shifting at the correct speed can be really boring. The reason many of us drive a standard shift sports car is to "rev" it up and shift by feeling, not by the numbers.

Some people are not emotionally prepared for the adventure of teaching someone to drive; that was my father hiding behind his newspaper as I tested his patience and threatened his existence. My wife, Linda, was not ready to teach our son to drive, so I got the pleasure of being the driving instructor. We went to a large, empty parking lot for our initial lesson and he did very well. He eventually learned enough to be a policeman and is now a detective.

You see, many people learn to drive a manual transmission because so many others are driving one. That is not the case with success in business; many people do not believe they are able to make it on their own. I hope to be a teacher who helps people to be successful in the business of their choice. I want to see them understand the mechanics, gain confidence and a "feel" for the journey, and then "rev it up" on life's highway.

Success in life and in business is a blend of many things, including but not limited to, information, skill, interest, mentors, friends, time, money, effort, good fortune and passion. Just as there are many different standard shift cars that have various clutch settings, there are many different ways to be successful in life and business. However, one thing never changes. You are guided by the Creator of the universe, who is the artist and scientist of your life. Always remember to make friends along the way and enjoy the journey!

To your success,

Lee Beard

Stories Of Transformation

The Secret to Enjoying Your Grand Life
Takahisa Iwamoto

We all know that death is inevitable. However, a lot of people do not believe that they will die. More accurately, people do not think about death. One day, I visited my business mentor, Hiroshi Tsukakoshi, CEO of Ina Food Industry Corporation at his office in Nagano, Japan. He is a well-known and financially successful business executive. I spent a few hours with him, and he shared many practical lessons from his own business experience and life lessons. The wisdom he shared has greatly influenced my business philosophy and strategies.

When our meeting was coming to a close, he told me he had something to give me. He handed me a large, poster-sized calendar and said, "I do not usually give this. It will be a life-changing gift for you if you are smart enough to know what it means. I call it the 100-year calendar because it shows all the dates from January 1, 2000, to December 31, 2100. If you look, you will see that there is an anniversary day of your death somewhere in this calendar."

I had never seen a calendar like it before. I wondered what he meant when he said it could be "life-changing" for me. I thought about the fact that the date of my death is in it. Death had never seemed real to me, even though I knew it was inevitable. The fact of my death drives me to think about how I want to live.

We must take life seriously. We are the owners of our lives. Every second is so precious that we must not waste it. We should be proud of what we do. If you have issues, face them directly and deal with them. If you do not know what to do, listen to the true voice that comes from your heart. Your conscience will tell you what to do.

Although it is not good to dwell on thoughts of dying, I do suggest that we reserve a day to consider it at least once a year. New Year's Day might be a good time to contemplate those things. But, why wait? Why don't you make today the day to consider your death seriously and decide how you want to live and use the time you have left? Your way of life and its purpose start at this moment. Design your grand life and enjoy it!

As you decide how you will design your future, I want you to think about something else. Did you know that humans are the only creatures that can smile? I do not know exactly why that is, but I believe that there is a reason for it. The smile is a magic tool that can bring happiness to us and to others. Your smile influences your surroundings. You should use this magic tool often, even when you may not feel like it!

When you are deciding how you will live, do things that you can smile about and try to make others smile.

My 100-year calendar is a reminder to me that life is short and uncertain. We should live each day with that in mind and try to live each moment to the fullest.

Takahisa Iwamoto

THE GOLDEN HOUR
Brian Tracy

You become what you think about most of the time. And the most important part of each day is what you think about at the beginning of that day.

Start Your Day Right
Take 30 minutes each morning to sit quietly and to reflect on your goals. You'll find when you read the biographies and autobiographies of successful men and women that almost everyone of them began their upward trajectory to success when they began getting up early in the morning and spending time with themselves.

Feed Your Mind With Positive Ideas
This is called the Golden Hour. The first hour sets the tone for the day. The things that you do in the first hour prepare your mind and set you up for the entire day. During the first thirty to sixty minutes, take time to think and review your plans for the future.

Use Your Quiet Time Effectively
Here are four things that you can do during that quiet time in the morning. Number one is to review your plans for accomplishing your goals and change your plans if necessary.

Number two is think of better ways to accomplish your goals. As an exercise, assume that the way you're going about it is totally wrong and imagine going about it totally differently. What would you do different from what you're doing right now?

Number three, reflect on the valuable lessons that you have learned and are learning as you move toward your goals.

Practice Daily Visualization
Number four, calmly visualize your goal as a reality. Close your eyes, relax, smile, and see your goal as though it were already a reality. Rewrite your major goals everyday in the present tense. Rewrite them as though they already existed. Write "I earn X dollars." "I have a net worth of X." "I weigh a certain number of pounds." This exercise of writing and rewriting your goals everyday is one of the most powerful you will ever learn.

Fasten Your Seatbelt
Your life will start to take off at such a speed that you'll have to put on your seatbelt. Remember, the starting point for achieving financial success is the development of an attitude of unshakable confidence in yourself and in your ability to reach your goals. Everything we've talked about is a way of building up and developing your belief system until you finally reach the point where you are absolutely convinced that nothing can stop you from achieving what you set out to achieve.

Everything Counts
No one starts out with this kind of an attitude, but you can develop it using the Law of Accumulation. Everything counts. No efforts are ever lost. Every extraordinary accomplishment is the result of thousands of ordinary accomplishments that no one recognizes or appreciates. The greatest challenge of all is for you to concentrate your thinking single-mindedly on your goal and by the Law of Attraction, you will, you must, inevitably draw into your life the people, circumstances and opportunities you need to achieve your goals.

Become A Living Magnet
Once you've mastered yourself and your thinking, you will become a living magnet for ideas and opportunities to become wealthy. It's worked for me and for every successful person I know. It will work for you if you'll begin today, now, this very minute, to think and talk about your dreams and goals as though they were already a reality. When you

change your thinking, you will change your life. You will put yourself firmly on the road to financial independence.

Action Exercises
Now, here are two things you can do every single day to keep your mind focused on your financial goals:

First, get up every morning a little bit earlier and plan your day in advance. Take some time to think about your goals and how you can best achieve them. This sets the tone for the whole day.

Second, reflect on the valuable lessons you are learning each day as you work toward your goals. Be prepared to correct your course and adjust your actions. Be absolutely convinced that you are moving rapidly toward your goals, no matter what happens temporarily on the outside. Just hang in there!

Brian Tracy

A Simple Act

Kris Zimmermann

It's amazing how a simple act can completely transform our lives. A few years ago, a couple of friends and I popped a video into the videocassette player to check out something interesting and new to us. The video was a Spring Forest Qigong (SFQ) exercise program about balancing energy in the body. We could really feel the energy. It started me on a path to uncover my "sleeping" talents.

As I continued to practice SFQ, my sensitivity to energy increased. I felt more energized and I began to have experiences helping friends and family and healing animals. As my heart opened wider, more love flowed through me and the energy started moving more quickly. It is a great feeling to actually help others by doing something I truly love.

In reality, I was doing something I loved before this big change; what I experience now is simply more expansive. I feel that I can do even more to help. I can now sense blocked energy and help clear excess energy. With love from the heart, a tremendous amount of energy can easily move.

Recently, I helped one of our horses after he suffered a puncture wound near his eye. I was so moved when he nuzzled me, thanking me for helping to relieve the pain and swelling. It was so beautiful that it made me cry!

On another occasion, I was able to offer support to a friend dying of cancer. I helped her find relief from the anxiety and pain, and she was able to move on peacefully. Life is full of beautiful experiences. There have been many similar situations since I discovered SFQ, all because my friends and I decided to explore something new. It's amazing what can unfold when you open yourself to something different.

SFQ has been so powerful that I have been drawn to explore other Learning Strategies programs, Diamond Feng Shui, Inner Diamond Feng Shui, and Dowsing. These programs have given me tremendous insight and support in awakening the many talents that I'm uncovering. It has made an incredible difference in my life, and I have been able to help so many others.

Sharing our knowledge, talents, and love is a wonderful and powerful way to help our world become more peaceful and abundant. I'm so grateful to all the people who have encouraged, influenced, and supported me in becoming who I am today. I'm honored to be working as a healer, helping others, sharing and doing what I can to create balance in the world. I'm grateful to God and the universe for helping me to live the life that I love. A simple act can change your world. I know, because one simple act surely changed mine!

Kris Zimmerman

Transformation and Inner Knowledge
René Blind

Looking back over the past 20 years, I realize my development and the people who came to me for help has been like a fairy tale. Let me tell you the story.

Once upon a time, a young student started his study in medicine and psychology at the University of Utrecht in the Netherlands. Soon, he became acquainted with homeopathy and other complementary medical activities like acupuncture, flower remedies, orthomolecular medicine and hypnotherapy, as well as the new creative visualization and manifestation techniques of Shakti Gawain. He realized in a very early stage of his study that the conservative regular medical and psychological paradigms are just belief systems that have profitable points and disadvantages, like every other belief system. After finishing his education at the university, he started a clinic for complementary medicine and psychology.

Through his years of study, he realized that all healing traditions have their own paradigms of good and bad. He realized that all patients and clients who came to him for help had their own individual healing paradigm. One could be helped through NLP, another through kinesiology, and another through homeopathy or cranio-sacral therapy. Others could be helped by conservative medical or psychological therapeutic interventions. Some couldn't be helped because none of the paradigms the doctor knew were the paradigms of the patients.

He recognized that the essence of the process of transformation and healing paralleled the patient's ability to attune and connect with his or her inner healer. The inner healer is the part of the unconscious self that knows the own rules of healing and the best way a person can be in harmony with him- or her-self and be healthy. John Upledger introduced this concept in his "cranio-sacral therapy." An example of the working of the inner healer occurred in a patient who could smell which orthomolecular medicines were good for her. As the inner healer was activated and the client became more connected with this part, the doctor could also establish a heart-mind connection with the patient, and miracles of healing transformation began to appear. In all the situations where he saw miraculous healings, there was a connection with the paradigms or belief systems within the client that allowed them to heal, just like a fairy tale.

As the doctor's years of work continued, it became clear that as more and more people lived in greater harmony with themselves, they were attracted to things that were beneficial to them. The doctor became aware of the fact that everyone needed to know their inner self at a deep level, and began stimulating this part of his clients and patients. Looking back, he understands that his way of working with the people who came to him for help transformed from diagnosing and treating to medical coaching. He wanted to stimulate and educate his patient's innate healing possibilities. He tried to stimulate them to see the infinite possibilities and learning capacities they had by empowering their inner wisdom. Through this process, they began to realize that they had given away their inner power and freedom, an action that often occurs in our modern society.

The importance of the connection of mind, body and spirit in order to heal physical, psychological and practical problems is often forgotten. There is always a connection between body, mind and spirit and therefore it does not matter where one begins to solve a problem; it is important to cure all three. By using training techniques to improve learning skills, one must continue to nurture the physical side as well. An example is taking breaks during a learning session in order to experience relaxation or to exercise. It is also important to take time to pray or meditate. People are healed physically as they learn how the body works and how to visualize and make contact with the inner healer. This allows them to pay attention to what their body is telling them.

In order to understand this more, the doctor delved deeper into his own inner wisdom. To prepare for this journey into his inner self, he looked for tools in the outer world and found them. The work of Paul Scheele and other members of Learning Strategies Corporation, the Sedona method, Gary Graig's Emotional Freedom Technique, the work of Deepak Chopra, and Sylvia Hartman's EmoTrance techniques are examples of some of these tools. As he listened to them, he heard himself speaking to his clients and patients, just as these teachers were speaking to him. He realized that even though he did not know these gifted authors in person, he felt connected to them. It was a circle to which he belonged, despite all spatial distances. He was surprised to discover that the material he learned about through courses from the U.S. was not known in the medical and psychological profession in the Netherlands.

His own quest in life appeared to be connected to the lives of the people who came to him for help. He realized our rational minds limit us to thinking that we journey alone.

He discovered that one of the red threads that stood out to him was goal setting. Goal setting is often accentuated for business opportunities, abundance strategies and sport. But goal setting is also a beacon of success in one's personal and family life, as well as physical and psychological health. These are areas that are easily damaged, but can be repaired through visualization and energy psychology techniques like the E.F.T. It seems humans have an innate desire to stay in their golden cage, even though the doors are open to freedom.

We forget that all people and things are connected to each other. If we try to stimulate the healing process and empower patients and clients who come to us for help, we also stimulate our own healing process, inner wisdom and quest for freedom. On the other hand, if we as healers, doctors and psychotherapists heal ourselves and become empowered and free, we will see our patients experience spontaneous healing.

In serving other people, we serve the world and ourselves. Essentially, there is no difference. By serving, we may all live "Happily Ever After."

René Blind

Manifest Your Life
Dianne Evans

By the time I left home as a teenager I was sucidial. I had learned it was best if I avoided people. They generally didn't like me and the feeling was mutual. In my twenties I worked at a job that was mentally and emotionally demeaning. My marriage was failing and I wanted to get a divorce. By the time I was divorced, my house was in foreclosure. I was miserable. Everything I touched seemed to go wrong. I was so depressed I could barely crawl out of bed to go to work. I didn't trust myself to do anything right and I never failed to live down to my opinion of myself.

One day I was very angry about something that had happened at work. As I was driving home, I slammed the dash of my car and swore that it was the only thing in my life that worked. Instantly, the car died! It was then I realized I was fabulous at manifesting anger, frustration, loss, and destruction. In fact I was one of the best manifesters I knew. I just didn't like what I was manifesting.

I studied what I was doing as well as what others did, to learn how we manifest things in our lives and then began to practice bringing about fun, love, excitement, and all of the things I wanted in my life. I learned that the pictures I made in my head and the words I chose to use were creating my world. I used to say that every time I saw a light at the end of the tunnel it turned out to be a train. I learned that every time I said that I created a train. It was like learning to speak a magic language. I learned how to consciously speak joy and excitement into my life instead of frustration and anger. My relationship with my family improved tremendously. Paul has stayed by me and taught me to laugh at myself and to see the best in people. Our California home is furnished with beautiful American and European antiques and we paid cash for a new pickup truck, SUV, and sports car.

Once I started understanding the method of manifestation, I began teaching others to manifest what they wanted in their lives as well. I love seeing friends transform their lives. I have a friend with muscular sclerosis who went from sitting in a wheel chair to walking to work. Another friend of mine had chronic fatigue and fibromyalgia and slept 18-20 hours per day. That friend is now able to return to a normal life. A friend with severe depression learned to have joy in her life and see the good in herself. Don't you want to know how to manifest what you want instead of what you've got? Now you can.

One night, I woke up in a frenzy and scribbled out an outline for my dream project, Magical University. It's a place of learning devoted to investigating the outer reaches of human potential; a place where I and many others join together to learn from each other. It is a place dedicated to conscious transformation.

I started with *Magical YOU!* After working on this for nearly two years I told my life coach, Sandi Amorim, that I had never really thought about writing or being an author, but, "It looks like I will be doing a lot of writing for all of the things I want to do. I could use some help being a prolific and entertaining author. I want what I write to be both educational and fun." Nine days later I received an invitation from Paul Scheele and Pete Bissonette to join as a co-author in this book. I know I am a manifester, but I was still shocked by the sudden response.

When I laid down to meditate on what I wanted to say, my meditation was interrupted...

The Parable of the Tomato

One day the tomato wakes up and realizes it's sitting in cowpucky. It's smelly, looks awful and is squishy. This, the tomato finds depressing. So it starts looking around growing over there and over here. But try as it might, everywhere it looks there is more cowpucky. The whole world is BS.

Now suicidal the tomato starts making up its own smelly stories. "I had bad parents and didn't go to the right schools. I'm no good. I'm not pretty and my health is bad." Eventually the tomato realizes that it is now contributing to the caca in the world and decides to add a dramatic touch. "No one will ever love me. Look at this pile of poop I'm in. Nothing I do ever turns out right."

Then the tomato figures out that making up bull can be interesting. So as long as it's making up stories, it might as well make up some good BS too. So the tomato starts talking about how its caca is rich and thick and warm. It has learned lots from all of the bull it's been through and at least its cowpucky grows some tasty tomatoes. And the tomato begins to manifest exactly what it is talking about.

Now, this tomato is a little more observant than your average tomato and wonders what would happen if it started to consciously choose the kind of stories it feeds on. So, I invite you to come try some of my cowpucky. My caca will warm you up; it will bring a smile to your face. My caca will make you laugh and maybe even bring you a friend. My caca doesn't stink, and if you use it, yours won't stink either.

And that's how transformation happens.

Dianne Evans

NEVER GIVE UP
Amanda Clarke

U ntil she was 24, her life fit together like a perfect jigsaw puzzle. As each piece connected, she climbed the ladder of success.

She ran her own business and doubled the company's income every year. Life was great; cost was never a concern. Property, automobiles, exclusive restaurants, expensive vacations: it seemed she had it all.

Then, she lost it all. Six years into the business, on a terrible day, her advisors counselled her to declare bankruptcy. There had been mounting debts and, thanks to the "head-in-the-sand" policy of denial she had assumed, the debts had grown to monstrous proportions—more than $468,000.

She remembers clearly the day her bubble of good fortune burst.

"I sat in the office at 9 p.m. with my head in my hands, and I sobbed," she said. "I knew the repercussions would be life-changing. I would have to terminate the employment of those who had been so loyal and faithful to me for many years. I would have to sell the home that I had bought for my mother some years earlier—leaving her homeless."

As she struggled to regain her composure that night, slowly but surely, she started working on a solution.

We'll examine her return from the fiscally dead, but let's first understand how she got into that situation.

She was an average schoolgirl; she didn't ignite any rockets in the educational system. Although she was a bright child, school didn't bring out the best in her and, at the age of 15, she left school to seek work and earn a living. She found that people warmed to her easily. Her first boss became a mentor who encouraged her to go to night classes and continue her education.

Three weeks before her 18th birthday she accepted the job of her dreams as a personal assistant to a company director. She was thrilled to accept the position, but soon became bored because the job lacked the challenge she expected. She re-evaluated her goals and aimed higher. Every job she applied for was offered to her.

By her 21st birthday, she knew that she wanted to run her own business and began making plans to do so.

Success knocked on her door from the onset. In the first year, in the midst of a recession, her new company made a profit of $22,500 and she had taken on her first employee. It seemed the sky was the limit; the company capitalized on its strengths, doubling turnover every year for 5 years. By the fifth year, she had two offices and seven employees and her confidence and reputation were soaring. Then, suddenly, she was like one of those cartoon characters who has run into a brick wall. Splat!

"My company began to flounder and its rapid growth diminished. There were warning signs, but I was in denial," she recalled ruefully. "Cash flow was incapable of covering the debts and, because I had chosen to bury my head in the sand, the debts were staggering."

In retrospect, that was probably the most extraordinary moment of her life. At the time, it was agony. She was overwhelmed by a myriad of emotions—self-pity, anger, frustration, a feeling of failure—but in the ashes of her crashed and burnt reality, there was a pulsating positive energy.

On that sorrowful day, as people partied in the street beneath her window, she burned the midnight oil, seeking a way to avoid bankruptcy and attack the problem aggressively. She explored many avenues of advice pertinent to her debt-laden situation.

From her library of about 5,000 titles she began pulling out any book that might hold the solution. There were books on debt management and finances, as well as biographies of the rich and famous like Richard Branson, Anita Roddick, Bill Gates, and Warren Buffet. She grew more certain by the minute that there was a way out. She decided on her goal, and in the following weeks and months, contacted each creditor and agreed on a payment. She started cutting back on resources, pinching pennies, and avoiding any unnecessary purchases—she even sold her executive car. Once the first creditor was paid off, she added that same monthly payment to the next creditor on her list, then on to the third, until all the creditors were paid in full.

Within one year of taking responsibility and control, she turned $68,000 of credit card debt into a $74,000 profit. Her mortgages of $253,000 and $42,000 were completely paid off only two and a half years later. By using financing and money managing techniques that are available, she went from being $390,000 in debt to having a positive bankroll of almost $74,000.

These days, once again, she can buy anything she wants and gets the opportunity to enjoy business-class travel, stays in some amazing places, and experiences exhilarating adventures that most can only dream of. She's been lost in a Peruvian jungle late at night, toured on independent safaris, enjoyed scuba-diving worldwide, jumped out of airplanes, flown in helicopters, and climbed mountains.

She has met and picked the brains of some of the most amazing people on this planet. She has become the author of several books and travels the world giving motivational speeches on how to get more out of your life and your career. And she has an impressive string of letters and credentials after her name: Amanda Clarke, MCIPD, MInstD, CPVA, CPBA, "Woman of the Year" as selected by the American Biographical

Institute, and "Cheshire in Business Award Winner."

If my personal story teaches anything, it's that sometimes life throws you a curve. Actually, sometimes life picks you up and throws you into a brick wall. At that point the big question is, "What do you do now?"

I know the answer to that question. You never quit. You are never beaten as long as you stay focused on the goal you want; not on failure. As long as you are determined and persistent, you will succeed. This is an amazing world that we live in, where opportunities abound like leaves falling off the trees in autumn. Seek out the opportunities; don't wait for them to find you. Make a list of your dreams and believe they are possible, focus on them and they will be yours – but you have to take action to make them happen! If you are in debt, set up a debt repayment plan, and focus on the financial goal you want to achieve. This same strategy also applies to other challenges in your life. Most of us have had to face such challenges in life, whether it's a poor background, abusive parents, drug abuse, failure at school, bad exam results, a car accident, or bad health.

The past is just a memory. It's what you do from this day forward that will determine who you really are.

Amanda Clarke

THE COURAGE TO DO IT...MY WAY
Sue Colvin

I sat down to write my story, like many others before me, with the desire to inspire someone to a life of greater joy and purpose. As I thought back over the past several years, I realized that, although many people have inspired and encouraged me, the most difficult thing for me was finding the courage to believe in myself and to do it my way.

December 2000 marked the beginning of an irrevocable change in my life. I was looking forward to the end of my career as an optometric technician and office manager. For 12 years I had worked for a dear man with whom I'd become great friends and we had formed a partnership—a special bond for life. He was looking forward to his retirement, while I was looking forward to a freedom that most people my age do not get to experience.

My husband, Dan, is a remarkable salesman and his excellence had not only afforded us trips to exotic places, but now allowed me to stay at home to pursue other interests I hadn't even thought of before! Life was good! Our daughter was expecting our first grandchild; we had one son in college and three more in the Air Force. I had thought long and hard about what I might like to do, given an opportunity, but I had no idea about any joyful hobby or pursuit. I only had the distinct feeling that something would come to me.

Suddenly, the bottom fell out from under us. My family seemed to be falling apart. The business my husband worked for was sold and business was going downhill fast. We were stressed to the extreme and I could see no other alternative but to go back out and get another job. Every fiber of my being fought that logical conclusion. I should have been willing to return to work, but I couldn't do it.

It was Christmastime, and I remembered the year before when I spent

Christmas Eve, our anniversary, in the hospital with my Dad after he had suffered a heart attack. I recalled the paralyzing fear that seared through me at the thought of losing him. Thank God the worst hadn't happened and he recovered.

Now, I was in the hospital again. This time I was standing next to my daughter who was in labor four months early. Nothing could be done and our first grandson died during birth. My husband said he could feel the life drain from my body as he held me up and we watched that little life slip away in heavy silence. It was at that moment that I realized I had no answers for my daughter when she asked me why God would let this happen. The entire foundation of my belief system since childhood crumbled. Only one thing remained with me and brought me through the pain. It was an incredible, powerful awareness of something greater than myself, greater than all of this pain. I felt that presence absolutely, without a doubt, in that room. I felt a sense of calm wash over me and a certainty of life after death.

I had been pouring my feelings in a journal over the previous two years, sure that at some point I would know what my purpose was. The day we brought our daughter home from the hospital, feeling empty, devastated and hopeless, I found my purpose. I sat down and began to write for the first time in my life. An outpouring of emotion came from somewhere beneath all of the pain, and words came together like a child's lullaby.

I was afraid to show my daughter what I had written for her because I was uncertain of her reaction. Would it help her, or would it hurt her more? I didn't know, but the words were from the deepest part of my heart and they were all I could give. I felt I could do no less than to honor that. It seemed to be of some comfort to her at a time where there was none. This is what I wrote:

In the dawn a child was born, though he didn't come to stay.

Wrapped in the tiniest blanket, in heavenly stillness he lay.
Through the tears and the sadness, came a message from above.
With each perfect little feature, this child came to us with love.
Though we cannot begin to explain, the reason for the sorrow and pain,
I feel his tiny presence say, "I will see you all again one day."
And so our lives have been touched, in such a wondrous awe,
By a little one who couldn't stay, he was a miracle baby after all.

The next year, the events of September 11th shook the world. Once again I felt the grip of fear as our youngest son was deployed to an undisclosed location, another son was placed on stand-by and a third son was sent to an Air Force base in a desert overseas. My mom was losing her health and her mind. I felt helpless and began pouring my feelings out on paper again.

Something happened while I was writing about life that allowed me to view things in a whole new light, and it gave me hope. I began to look for something good to come out of the hard times, even when there was nothing in sight. That little bit of hope seemed to be something to hang on to, and sure enough, many things turned around. It did not always happen the way I expected; in fact it rarely did. Nonetheless, it was good—at times even magical.

Since then, I have written when emotion and compassion inspire me. People have been generous with their support and response, especially my husband and family. But inside, there is a great deal of fear: fear of rejection and fear of not being good enough. I have continued to write from my heart, but I have not had the courage to take the next step. I am taking it now.

Since that first poem, I have had to do it my way. I have to write from that place of authentic self and go with what comes to me.

What I consider to be the most valuable realization is that my own guidance—that power that is greater than myself but not separate from myself—is always available to me. It helps me find the courage to honor my convictions. It is the power that gently urges me to stay in the moment, no matter how much fear appears to have a hold on me. That power has seen my family and me through to much better times. I am indeed living the life I love!

Follow your passion, whatever it takes and wherever it leads you, and trust your inner self to show you the way.

Sue Colvin

A PASSION FOR GIVING:
THE ANTHONY ROBBINS FOUNDATION
Anthony Robbins

Global Impact

The Anthony Robbins Foundation was created in 1991 with the belief system that, regardless of stature, only those who have learned the power of sincere and selfless contribution experience life's deepest joy: true fulfillment. The Foundation's global impact is provided through an international coalition of caring donors and volunteers who are connecting, inspiring and providing true leadership throughout the world!

Global Relief Efforts

The Anthony Robbins Foundation offers its heartfelt compassion to the victims of the numerous natural disasters felt throughout the world. The Foundation is passionate about participating in the coordination of reconstruction activities and evaluates funding requests on an ongoing basis. As men and women affected by these disasters begin to rebuild, the Anthony Robbins Foundation takes honor in providing hope and funding support to the many suffering communities.

Adopt-A-School Program, New Orleans, USA

Katrina Relief Efforts continue to be a focus of the Foundation. The Foundation will support the rebuilding efforts throughout the Gulf Coast through a partnership with its Youth Mentoring Program partner, Communities In Schools (CIS). CIS is the nation's leading community-based stay-in-school network, connecting needed community resources with schools. CIS has over thirty-four chapters serving well over 2 million children nationally. The Foundation will focus on rebuilding the educational infrastructure currently affecting thousands of children in Louisiana, Mississippi, and Alabama.

The Foundation is proud to announce its partnership with the Adopt-A-School Program in New Orleans to support the rebuilding efforts of

STORIES OF TRANSFORMATION

Ben Franklin Elementary. This elementary school was the first public school to open in New Orleans post-Katrina. Ben Franklin Elementary is operating near its capacity by serving 555 students, a 24% increase in student population since Hurricane Katrina. Over 90% of its students reside in high poverty households. The Foundation will provide funding and hands-on assistance toward rebuilding the library, playground and other structural needs. The Foundation's goal is to provide the funds and tools necessary to transform this elementary school into an enhanced learning environment.

Adopt-A-School Program, The Citizens Foundation, Pakistan
The Anthony Robbins Foundation will provide support to The Citizens Foundation which manages many relief programs in Pakistan, rebuilding schools and homes following the earthquake on October 8, 2005. It is widely recognized that, because of crumbling schools, the children suffered the greatest blow from the October quake. It has been reported that some 10,000 schools collapsed throughout Pakistan. The Anthony Robbins Foundation is proud to support the construction of a 6,500 square foot school in the Bagh district of Kashmir, Pakistan. Upon completion, this school will serve 180 students during the academic year beginning in April 2007.

Hebron Orphanage, India
Over the past 40 years, Hebron Orphanage has saved homeless orphans from dying of starvation on the streets of southern India. These orphaned children have been given love, life and a future. The Anthony Robbins Foundation adopted Hebron Orphanage following the 2004 Tsunami. The orphanage has expanded its facilities and now accommodates 400 children. The Foundation is delighted to provide funding to support Hebron Orphanage's immediate need to build a new stand-alone boy's dormitory, enabling the number of male residents to increase to 100, and to allow the current boy's dormitory to be used as a library and classrooms.

Langfang Children's Village, Beijing China

The Langfang Children's Village in Beijing, China was founded to support mainland China's orphaned and special needs children. Many children come to the village because they are abandoned at the front gates or brought to the Langfang by locals. It is home to more than 90 orphans from approximately ten different orphanages scattered throughout China. China is working hard at improving the plight of these children, but as a developing country with over 5 million orphans, the problem is simply too large.

The Langfang Children's Village is designed to model a normal family environment and de-emphasizes the institutional feel often associated with orphanages. Every child lives in a freestanding home with house parents and their own yard to play in. The Anthony Robbins Foundation provides funding to the Langfang Children's Village to support the daily needs of the children, as well as medical treatment at an on-location clinic. This collaborative effort is contributing to the well-being of these beautiful children, allowing the Foundation to work toward fulfilling its mission of global impact.

Global Community Connection Day

The Anthony Robbins Foundation proudly sets aside one day a month to proactively connect with non-profit organizations throughout the world. Its goal is to meet the challenges of a global community, come up with solutions and TAKE ACTION! We visit and provide in-kind donations to schools, hospitals, and shelters for the homeless to nurture, feed and mentor those in need. Recently, the Foundation supported the Children's Hospitals of San Diego and New Orleans with donations of stuffed bears for their in-patients. The Foundation also supported the Diabetes Association in their annual Tour de Cure cycling event held in San Diego and Santa Monica, California in honor of the National Physical Fitness and Sports Month.

Anthony Robbins

The Dream-Catcher Trail
AmyLee, Medicine Woman

THE PROPHECY: "The Systems by which we define ourselves transform from the number 7 to 12... 7 Colors of the Rainbow... 7 notes of the musical scale... the 7 energy wheels (chakras), 7 Directions, and so on, shall all become systems of 12...then 13..."

The invitation to contribute to this book came the day the powers that (think they) be were re-determining the current number of planets in our solar system. In one determination, we actually had 12 planets! Twenty-four hours later and the "re-re-definition" took 3 steps backward. Pluto "bit the cosmic dust" and our solar system was re-Transformed to 8 planets.

The birth of a new era does not dawn evenly on all in the same moment. It comes with starts and stops, illuminations and shadows — the proverbial two steps forward and just as many back, and a few steps sideways. One measure of personal, global, even galactic Transformation is one's ability to discern which way one is moving.

The Old Medicine Woman slumped back in the faded vinyl passenger seat of her Apprentice's new old Pontiac. **Red Light.** Both engine and Indians were idling.

The Old One had reached her limit — seeing one too many of those little "Dream Catchers" twirling from rear view mirrors. "What's with people?" she began her pagan sermonette. "We gift them corn to save their skinny bones, and they *transform* it into liquor that kills our people, and addictive corn syrup that's robbing their own youth of their vital health. We gift them sacred Tobacco, which, by the way, never gave one Indian cancer in 40,000 years....until they *transformed* it into poison sticks."

Green Light. She, and Pontiac, were on a roll! "We gifted them the prototype for their government, and they *transformed* it from the pure democracy we Iroquois have into a... good old white boys' club. We *gifted*, no, we didn't gift them our continent...but they sure *transformed* that too."

Outside Limits. The rusty old automobile and the crusty Old Woman took off with a roar. "And then, just when I thought it was safe for you, Granddaughter, to go out into the world on our behalf, and share the Earth-Walking, Spirit-Talking Ways with them, to teach them *respectful* ways to honor the Dream-Medicine...what did they do with our Gift? They *transformed* it into mass-imported plastic Dream-Catchers dangling from every rear view mirror!"

Yield. (The Last Granddaughter knew to just keep her eyes on the road and her ears, heart, and mind open to this Old Woman's Wisdom, even the parts that made her squirm.)

Caution Light; everyone slowed down.
Well, almost everyone.

"And another thing, what's with this "*Pontiac*?" What do you think Chief Pontiac would have to say about how they *transformed* his honor into a man-made money-making gas-guzzling earth-robbing, metal machine?"

(The Last Granddaughter hoped the Old Iroquois hadn't noticed the four balding *Mohawk Tires* spinning under her.)

Curve Ahead.
Spicy Old Wit hit again. "Oh look, a whole village of Jeep *Cherokees*! And they say we're a *vanishing* race?"

A soft chortle trickled from the Old One's breath and mingled with the echoing image of her youth, sitting next to her. "Here's my point,

Granddaughter: we give them Gifts to *transform* some aching part of their lives, to fill an empty belly or hungry soul, and no matter how hard we try, they just don't get the Real Gift. They are so busy *transforming* its symbols into empty adornments, only perpetuating precisely that which created their hunger in the first place."

STOP.
Somebody hit the brakes.

Passing Lane.
She leaned back to better see the One-who-was-next-following-her-steps, this Last Granddaughter in the Medicine Lineage, "So, what do you think, Next Generation?" And, she really truly, with her whole old heart, listened.

Soft Shoulder.
Thinking back over the coast-to-coast Dream-Catcher nightmare, the Granddaughter re-witnessed their gaudy displays on hotel walls and reservation casinos, in grimy gas stations, dangling from waitresses' pierced ears and rear view mirrors, and heaped, along with flip-flops and jelly bracelets, in steep discount close-out bins. "Well, I think it's most symbolic, that a people who continue to sleep-walk through their lives would display their Dream-Catchers everywhere they go. At least it's honest – they advertise right up front that they aren't yet awake, aren't yet conscious."
"Hmh." The Old One nodded.
"Hmh." The One-day-Old-One nodded back.

Signal. Old attitude *transformed*. Pontiac turned. Engine stopped. Home again. Safe and sound.

"Transformation" is happening constantly; in the seed itching its way through the Earth's skin, toward the Light it seeks, in every cell of our own bodies as they continually die, renew and die again. Transformation is

everywhere – from the silky butterfly cocoon to the stinky bison dung. We are all on a Journey somewhere and the vehicle is Transformation. Just getting to "Here" and "Now" required astounding Transformation! Wherever you go next will be comprised of nothing less. Life's definition embodies ongoing Transformation. It is not Transformation itself that we seek; rather, it is how we think Transformation will make us feel differently about our lives. I am not qualified to speak on the quality of another's Transformation, as both the cocoon and the bison dung perfectly serve their myriad purposes.

Transformation can present us with Free-Will Choice: The choice to move through the experience with which we are presented, with Love, or with Fear. Select (consciously or not) which vehicle you will ride, Love or Fear, and the next leg of your continual Transformation trip is set. Choose one, and you get to ride up on the road; scenic, sometimes marked, a few chuckholes, roadside rests, and good companions and annoying drivers. Choose the other, and you'll still get your Transformation, you'll still get to where you're going, as even the craggiest ditch runs parallel to the road.

Who am I to speak of such travels? I am that Last Granddaughter who criss-crossed the continent for over three decades, sharing the Wisdom of my Elders, and their Dreams for our collective Future.

To you-who-are-open to receiving the Meaning of the Gifts my Lineage offers, I extend my open hand and heart. To those whose chosen trails brush mine but briefly, I honor you – offering, and accepting, respect for our different paths. And, to those who choose to sleepwalk their way through what must seem an endless, often fearful, night, I wish you but the Sweetest Dreams, and a waiting Sun and Moon for when You rise – and Shine!

The Prophecy's interpretation continues: "Include the black keys on the piano, the musical scale transforms from 7 to 12 notes. Count the 'new' colors where the Rainbow's 7 touch, then blend. Embrace the anchor of Earth, and the Ethers in which our minds travel, and our so called "chakras" grow in number. All these, and more, have been there all along. They have not changed. Transformation is found not in the evolution of external objects and events, but in the evolving internal awareness, acceptance, alignment of the observer."

AmyLee, Medicine Woman

EMBRACE SILENCE
Dr. Wayne Dyer

You live in a noisy world, constantly bombarded with loud music, sirens, construction equipment, jet airplanes, rumbling trucks, leaf blowers, lawn mowers and tree cutters. These manmade, unnatural sounds invade your senses and keep silence at bay.

In fact, you've been raised in a culture that not only eschews silence, but is terrified of it. The car radio must always be on, and any pause in conversation is a moment of embarrassment that most people quickly fill with chatter. For many, being alone in silence is pure torture.

The famous scientist Blaise Pascal observed, "All man's miseries derive from not being able to sit quietly in a room alone."

With practice, you can become aware that there's a momentary silence in the space between your thoughts. In this silent space, you'll find the peace that you crave in your daily life. You'll never know that peace if you have no spaces between your thoughts.

The average person is said to have 60,000 separate thoughts daily. With so many thoughts, there are almost no gaps. If you could reduce that number by half, you would open up an entire world of possibilities for yourself. For it is when you merge into the silence, and become one with it, that you reconnect to your source and know the peacefulness that some call God. It is stated beautifully in Psalms, "Be still and know that I am God." The key words are "still" and "know."

"Still" actually means "silence." Mother Teresa described the silence and its relationship to God by saying, "God is the friend of Silence. See how nature (trees, grass) grows in silence; see the stars, the moon and the sun—how they move in silence. We need silence to be able to touch souls." This includes your soul.

It's really the space between the notes that makes the music you enjoy so much. Without the spaces, all you would have is one continuous, noisy note. Everything that's created comes out of silence. Your thoughts emerge from the nothingness of silence. Your words come out of this void. Your very essence emerged from emptiness.

All creativity requires some stillness. Your sense of inner peace depends on spending some of your life energy in silence to recharge your batteries, remove tension and anxiety, thus reacquainting you with the joy of knowing God and feeling closer to all of humanity. Silence reduces fatigue and allows you to experience your own creative juices.

The second word in the Old Testament observation, "know," refers to making your personal and conscious contact with God. To know God is to banish doubt and become independent of others' definitions and descriptions of God. Instead, you have your own personal knowing. And, as Meville reminded us so poignantly, "God's one and only voice is silence."

Dr. Wayne Dyer

The Open Door
Dr. Marilyn Robinson

Slowly my eyes opened as I awoke, lying on the floor. I felt as though a crushing weight was bearing down on me. As my eyes focused, I remembered where I was and the events of the past 48 hours. It was 5 o'clock in the morning, the day after I said goodbye to my soul mate, best friend, lover, and husband, for the last time. Our office was my chosen area of retreat, the folded blankets offering some comfort from the carpeted floor, firm and strong below my prone body. Some force, beyond my own capabilities, caused me to rise from the spot on the floor where I had slept for three brief hours. I knew what I had to do. I sat at the computer and composed an email to communicate the unspeakable to our friends and family—my husband, the center of my world, was deceased. Frank, who had been so vibrant, joyous, healthy, loving, and fascinated by life, was gone. There was much that needed to be planned and done before the light of day. So, while family members slept, I began the journey of life without Frank.

As I went through the motions of composing emails and making a list of things that needed to be done, I knew that a force stronger than myself kept me going after what had been an earth-shattering two days. In his departure from this world, Frank had given the gift of life to three people through organ donations. He also gave me the gift of certainty that I would survive the free fall that threatened to engulf me. I felt tremendous gratitude for the years I had with Frank, and that gratitude lifted my heart and carried me through the days of funeral preparation, burial, and life without him. I wanted to mourn him, to cry out in anguish, to retreat to a place within myself where the hard reality of life without my beloved would not touch me. But I knew that to do any less than live life to the fullest would be no tribute to the man I loved so dearly. To be less than a source of strength for everyone who loved him so much would be to deny all the things that I had learned as a result of our years together.

It was true that my life would never be the same, but the sensation in my heart refused to allow me to dwell on the loss of Frank. Rather, an urgent need grew within me to understand why I had been so lucky to have him in my life; to discover why we fit like two intricate pieces. Perhaps if I could unfold the mysteries of our relationship, I would find a greater purpose to our lives, and to my life without him. Thus began my intense search for self-discovery and understanding of things beyond my current level of awareness and comprehension.

My emotions have rebelled at times, pulling me down a path of loss, self-pity, loneliness, and fear. As quickly as this lesser self tries to take hold of me, the image of Frank enters my mind and I know I have much to learn and to contribute as a result of our life together. Gratitude takes the place of grief, life takes the place of reclusion, and a need for certainty is replaced with a passion to discover what door has opened to allow the discovery of my true purpose in life.

As second oldest child, and first girl in a family of twelve children, I was blessed with parents who showed strength, optimism, and unconditional love in the most trying circumstances. I learned we don't have to be with someone to know and experience the love of that person. While most of us have moved from the place where we lived as children, we retain the closeness that integrated our lives while growing up. Another lesson learned was, in death, to celebrate and cherish the memories of our loved one, knowing they continue to guide and be with us even after their physical presence is long gone. I learned a pattern of dealing with loss with the death of Tommy, one of my brothers, in 1990. First, acknowledge the loss and recognize it for what it is, no more and no less. Next, focus on what you have to be grateful for, the many wonderful memories and experiences. Last, as my father loved to say, "get back up on the horse" and move forward. That is exactly what we did when my beloved father died, six months after Frank's departure from this world.

I had known Frank, through work, for many years. I knew him as a kind, funny, generous, intelligent, and hard-working person. His first wife, Betty, had died from cancer in 1991. I had been divorced since 1984. During daily walks to and from a business conference in the spring of 1994, we learned more about each other and a friendship began to develop. Within a few months, Frank told me that he was falling in love with me and he hoped it wouldn't hurt our newly formed friendship. I did not have the same feelings, but I valued our friendship and told him so. When I awoke the next morning, it was like a lightening bolt had struck me. I knew that I loved Frank and that he was the one I was supposed to be with for the rest of my life. Over dinner that night I proposed that we get married. Two weeks later, on a beautiful Sunday afternoon in August 1994, we became husband and wife.

Perhaps the lesson is that when we open our heart to another, without expectations, love happens. It has been said that soul mates have a connection that lasts for a lifetime and that the connection provides an opportunity to learn very important lessons. What happens if we close the door to that lesson upon the loss of our loved one? What gift are we shutting out? What life-changing awareness and understanding are we walking away from? What other losses will we experience until the lesson is learned? Perhaps the most important lesson that I've learned since Frank's death is that there is always more love than we think. To access this abundance of love, we must forsake the belief that we know all we need to know, that what we have is as good as it gets, and that connecting with ourselves is more important than connecting with others.

I live in amazed gratitude for those who have been there for me: my mother, the incarnation of love and my role model; the family, friends, and business associates who have allowed me into their lives and who have shared their sweet, humorous, and cherished memories of Frank;

and mentors, like Tony Robbins, who have shared their thoughts, inspiration, and knowledge. Such people are there for you, too. Open the door and walk into their love; open your heart and walk into life.

Dr. Marilyn Robinson

Epiphany
Roxey Lau

How can I ever forget that day? It marked the dawn of my epiphany, a major turning point in my life. That was the day I consciously chose to assume responsibility for and ownership of my life, and I knew there was no turning back. On that cold but sunny day on February 6, 1989, I was a Chinese-American living in Munich, Germany, tossing confetti at the crowd at Marienplatz on Carnival Shrove Tuesday.

Two months before, I had completed my assignment as Income Director of The Hunger Project Germany by reaching their 1988 target income of over $400,000—the highest annual income in their history until 2005. This was an important step in funding the end of hunger on the planet. And yet I was feeling burned out, empty, and "hungry"— devoid of joy, fulfillment and satisfaction. To accept this post, I had closed down the Hunger Project office in Luxembourg, given up my flat, sold my car, and hopped on a plane to get to Munich as quickly as possible. My German life partner followed me, and we were ensconced in a wonderful flat in the city center.

The moment they found out I was no longer working for The Hunger Project, the German government gave me exactly four days to leave the country. They saw no further reason for me to stay since I was not allowed to take a job that could be performed by a German citizen and I was not allowed to marry my German life partner without a birth certificate (this document, among others, was lost when my parents moved to the United States). As I did not want to leave Munich—now my only home—I immediately applied for a student visa to buy some time and hire a lawyer to help me secure a permanent residence permit.

Prior to my involvement with The Hunger Project, I had merely worked to earn money at a series of odd jobs that included secretarial, administrative, and middle-managerial positions for various corporations and financial institutions. These jobs served no purpose other than getting paid. They were almost — without exception — without passion, without heart, without vision, and required little more than going through the motions for survival purposes. On that day I decided that, from now on, I would never again sell out for money (or love and approval, for that matter). My mind was racing in many directions in search of a solution, contemplating other options and possibilities, refusing to give in to the present reality, which looked increasingly bleak. I had no money put aside and didn't know how I was going to financially get through the month of February.

In this state of nearly unbearable tension and fertile chaos, some important "what-if" questions popped into my mind. What if I were to manage to find a way to remain in Munich, a city I had grown to love? What if I were to create my own business and manage to be financially self-sufficient while doing something I enjoyed—a career that represented who I am, that would be worthy of me, that would afford me growth and fulfillment, while allowing me to contribute to the quality of life on the planet? What if I were able to make myself free from paid employment forever? While I had no idea how this would come about, I was clear that this was exactly what I wanted. In this state of not-knowing, of insecurity, and hope-free choicelessness, came the greatest freedom I had ever known—the freedom to choose what I wanted to do and how I wanted to live.

After The Hunger Project, I wanted to somehow continue working to end "hunger," but in a way that addressed the spiritual, emotional and intellectual aspects of life. At that time, I was fortunate enough to have a couple of friends whom I had successfully coached in personal matters. Those friends served as messengers of my subconscious and encouraged me to seriously consider coaching professionally. It was the perfect time to take a leap. And when I did, I don't think I had ever felt more powerful, free, sure and alive. This meant taking full responsibility for my life and not having the convenience of blaming circumstances, events, or other people if things didn't turn out—and things not turning out was definitely not an option. It was either shape up (create my own life and become self-sufficient) or ship out (leave Germany and admit defeat).

For the next five days, I deliberately dove into a sea of creative turmoil, running the whole gamut of emotions from anxiety, exasperation, desperation, inadequacy, and doubt to exhilaration, elation, enthusiasm, determination, and a deep inner knowing until MY VISION EMERGED! I was quietly and profoundly moved by it. It felt authentic, natural, true, worthy of me and deeply personal. It was simply this: to support individuals to live a life of power, passion and purpose. I wanted to be the catalyst, the oracle, the mirror for their awakening, consciousness and expansion. I wanted to be a compassionate and committed listening for their love, power, vision, gifts and greatness to emerge. I wanted to support people to grow up to be who they really are, to ask ever more relevant and empowering questions, to embrace change and, if necessary, to fall apart to a truer foundation. My clients are my best teachers; it is their courage and deep commitment to self that has made my work, and who I am today, possible.

As I was one of the very first life coaches in Germany, and as there were no existing Lifestyle Designers (as I then called myself), I was finally allowed to stay in Germany, but only on the condition that I confined myself to this one line of work and none other, which suited me just fine. I ended up getting plenty of press, a radio interview, my own column in a spiritual magazine over a two-year period, and my "15 minutes of fame." I have now been coaching for 17 years and would feel quite privileged to do it for the rest of my life since it's what I'm truly passionate about! I am immensely grateful that the universe conspired to push me in this direction.

I strive to teach what I intimately know: being precedes doing, breakdown precedes breakthrough, and passion precedes pay. Create your own distinction and do your own thing. Be audacious enough to name the "what," and the "how" will reveal itself in its own perfect speed. Embrace change as a vital part of being alive, of growing and expanding. I make up every part of this work as I go, to ensure that it is relevant, alive and true. From individual sessions to business development to seminars, including a five-day men's retreat, all aspects of my work involve an invitation to awaken one's full potential and the courage to stand one's true ground.

Within my first month of work I had twelve clients. I was told at the outset that it would be very difficult to make a living with this, but I'm still here and I intend to be for a very long time as I continue to learn and grow and thrive. I can ask for no greater blessing. I will continue to do this work as if lives and souls depended on it. I trust that I will always have clients committed to personal evolution, who demand a supportive, compassionate, creative, objective and respectful listening who takes in all that they are while they create their lives out of their own truth, freedom, and deepest vision of self and of humanity.

Roxey Lau

WAKE UP TO LIVE THE LIFE YOU LOVE
Jan Balling Frederiksen

My Intention
I have always known that there was a new crusade to be on, but I needed to decide which one would fulfill the body, mind and spirit in others and myself.

Perhaps this story will be one of the most important stories for others who are on a similar crusade as myself. These are the people who want to assist in helping other business leaders find their true purpose for the benefit of mankind. They want to create a way to help all of us have a life filled with happiness, relaxation and meaning.

Others on a similar crusade have become obsolete business models. Their era has not brought us fulfillment, freedom, peace, harmony or acceptance of diversity—at best, their era brought about a more stressful life for others.

I want to explore ways to find the Business Knight inside me and help others do the same. But, you may ask, *What is a business knight?*

The Credo of a Business Knight
I believe that global businesses have the power and money to make a significant difference in today's troubled world. By making that difference they will help themselves as well as others. I envisage business men and women who raise their sights higher than the bottom line, who allow their work to become a vocation like higher professions. In order to make this possible, I believe businesses must add a moral dimension to their agenda and become more service and value-oriented by eliminating the assumed natural distinction between private enterprise and public institutions. I picture businesses taking responsibility for the world in which they operate and creating wealth for it. I see myself becoming one of those "servant leaders"—not merely

a stockholder, colleague, and employee servicing customers and products. I want to help my community, the planet, humanity, the future and life itself.

I'm sure you have a lot of questions. Let me begin to answer them by telling you a little about myself and how I have come to be where I am now.

My History in Brief

I am a 51-year-old husband and father from Denmark who has learned to be proud of my heritage and the small country I call home. People from the cold, northern part of Europe can influence the world in ways both good and bad. I come from a hard-working family. My father died when I was four—I thought. He was not my biological father though. I have never seen my biological father. He was a nature-guy who worked in the Swedish forests. However, as I grew into puberty, my mother looked at me and said I looked more and more like her only true love. That fact could have spared me a lot of pain and suffering I had endured since the age of four. My mother was a strong woman with good values, who always took good care of me, and we had a telepathic link.

I had a school teacher who became a father-figure to me. I finished school and had no other opportunity available to me other than entering the workforce—so that's what I did. I studied information technology in the evenings beginning at the age of 16. It was not until much later in life that I began to really study and I received my bachelor's degree and took MBA exams.

I met my first wife at the age of 16 and had two sons by the time I was 24-years-old. We divorced later because I spent too much time building my first company of information technology consultants between the ages of 28 and 32. By the time I was 36, I was remarried with two more children.

I have always tried to live my life in the order of these standards: Be happy, have fun, make a difference, be profitable. But somehow these standards started to turn upside down, until profitability was my only focus and inner happiness moved to the back burner. I still lived a good life and worked hard. There was love, happiness and materialism. Then, in 2002, it all crashed, and I became very depressed.

I have been a leader for many years in different companies. My most recent position was as a global partner and consultant. I worked with national and international companies. From time to time, I felt ill-at-ease in many of the situations I found myself. I was often uncertain of whether or not I was in the right place at the right time. In most cases, I learned to accept things as they were. But other times, I could not accept them. I sometimes tried different routes—some were successful and others weren't—and I learned from these experiences.

One of these different routes took place in 2002 after a tough—and fun—5 year period of time when I worked for one of five large international management consulting businesses. There were lots of downs and only a few ups.

As a result, I broke off and began my own company that would train other leaders to use the seven habits described in Steven R. Covey's book *The Seven Habits of Highly Effective People*. I co-invested and brought my franchise to the Nordic market—but I soon felt restricted by the concept. Then everything crashed again, and events in my own life forced me to look deep into myself. I practically had to re-invent myself and my roles as a father, husband and business man. It took the help of doctors, psychologists, spiritual guides, hypnosis guides, chiropractors, body therapists, old friends and others. It was a trying period for my wife and sons and I thank them a lot for their patience. But as my wife, Vibeke, says, "I can accept you doing crazy things, as long as you are happy."

As the saying goes, "If you want to change the world, start with yourself." And that's what I did. Now I feel more at ease and more alive than I ever have before. I can actually feel the energy level in my body for the first time in 20 years.

After 4 years of learning and reading all that I could get my hands on, I know I am ready for a big jump—and a new mission—the mission of now—a result of my inner wake-up call.

I have worked in many different settings with different angles. Just recently an epiphany came to me based on an inspirational article from Danah Zohar. I realized we all should aim for a new role model in the world, one that is similar to the old world with all the glamour that came with it. In other words, we should all aim to be Business Knights. In my world of words, this is the best metaphor to express a win-win mindset and synergistic thinking and doing.

I wrote an introductory letter about becoming a Business Knight and submitted it to Danah Zohar in order to apply for a seat in her new course, *Spirituality in Organizations*, and I was able to meet with her in Amsterdam. We really connected and I have been invited to join her inner-management circle to create the first call for Business Knights, which begins in August 2007. I am happy that I found the courage in my heart to dare to take the steps that brought me here.

I am ready for the power of now; are you?

How to find and become a Business Knight
The Business Knight concept is a new way for me to give back all of the good things I have received from others in my life. I have been privileged enough to get what I asked for, even though it was hard at times. I believe that you can achieve what you want. I also believe if you don't die, you will be strengthened—according to evolutionary theory. As Monty Python would say, "Life is a bitch and then you die."

I believe I am on a new crusade, and I want to invite others to join me. We can allow our ambitions to come from within, leave our egos at the door, and set out to conquer the world as a part of the new global world of Business Knights. I urge you to join us in creating a movement of networks and organizations that will find, train, measure and celebrate these Business Knights as a method of achieving a new work environment that focuses on sustaining others as well as our world.

I encourage you to accept this invitation to participate in the first inspirational workshop where we will work initially to establish a "Knight's Global Impact Day" that will take place each year. This is a day where everyone will serve as a knight in the area of their choice and help us all to create a better world both for businesses and communities.

Jan Balling Frederiksen

STORIES OF TRANSFORMATION

THE FLIGHT WITH FACELESS ANGELS
Randall R. Sevenish, Esq.

Well before my transformation, my wife Jeanie, a farmer's daughter, learned about hard work at an early age. To this day it amazes me how she transforms from a "morning-'til-night-digging-in-the-dirt-in-her-huge-garden, taking-care-of-our-animals" caterpillar into a stunning and beautiful, blond butterfly. Aside from caring for and attracting God's creatures to our dream home on seven acres, she has always been there for me and our daughters, Alyssa and Abby, over the years. I have seen her save the lives of animals when the vet had given up. She was always an inspiration for my daughters and me whenever any of us encountered inevitable life struggles.

Jeanie supported my decision to return to college early in our marriage while I was a police officer and she was a teacher at a school for the deaf. She supported me in my decision to go to law school and made adjustments at home. She supported me in my decision to open martial arts schools in which our black-belt daughters worked with us, allowing us, as a family, to touch many lives. She supports me in my injury law practice, in which she is an intricate part. Her entire life has been selflessly dedicated to supporting her family, making sacrifices, seemingly taking a back seat. In reality, she has always been the driver without ever realizing it. With Jeanie's backing, I was able to accomplish many things I was very proud of: being a police officer, SWAT Commander and drill instructor at the academy, being named Officer of the Year by the City of Indianapolis, black-belt degrees in Karate, the positive impact we had upon the lives of Karate students and police, getting into and then completing law school, and having a successful law practice. Until my transformation, I had taken all that for granted.

One morning, she had accumulated fluid in her body overnight and was visibly swollen all over. Her kidneys had shut down due to what turned out to be Lupus. One day I brought her home from a Lupus-related hospital stay when she was the most ill. I assisted her into the shower, staying close by. She fearfully yelled my name and as I pulled back the shower curtain, she trusted that I would catch her. She became limp in my arms and I placed her on our bed. I realized, as I looked into her eyes, that my wife, soul-mate, and best friend, had just died in my arms—her spirit had instantly left. With a stoic face, I silently screamed, "No! This cannot be so! This is not happening!"

In that split second I was transformed by the realization of how unimportant everything else was. All of my accomplishments—our beautiful home, my plans for the future—were all meaningless without her. I realized in an instant that the most wonderful human being I had ever been privileged to know had suddenly died in my arms! As a former police officer, I knew firsthand the appearance of death, and I knew she—her spirit—had left.

Surprisingly, I didn't panic. I calmly, perhaps numbly, dialed 911. I reported in a firm, confident voice, *"My wife is not breathing. I need an ambulance—now!"* Although I didn't know this for several weeks, my voice had also been heard thundering through the heavens. Apparently, my voice not only sounded thunderous but also pitiful, because it was heard by my wife and the two faceless angels who were at that instant in the process of escorting Jeanie to heaven. She may have heard my confident voice but knew I was about to be crushed.

Even though she was happier in that moment than she had ever been, she knew she had a choice. She knew she could continue with the angels to heaven, or return to this much less-than-perfect world and to her husband. As usual, she thought of someone else first. Rather than letting go and being happy to be back home with the Lord and other family, friends, and animals, she thought, *"Poor Randy. He is so pitiful. I can't do this to him."* I hung up the phone and went to unlock the door for the medics. As I returned to Jeanie with plans of starting CPR, she suddenly sat up in bed and began cursing like a sailor.

What startled me was not the cursing, but that she was back! I could hardly believe my eyes. She continued to bark commands at me and complain that she could hear my conversation with 911—how dare I call for an ambulance when she had no clothes on! Tears welled up in my eyes, as they do each time I think about this transformational event. I was so happy to have found a reason to laugh. And laugh out loud I did. Jeanie is back! She didn't leave me and the Lord confirmed in her return, "Not yet!"

It seemed as though hours had gone by between her calling me from the shower and her "return." In fact, only a few minutes had gone by in time as we know it. In those few minutes of human time, Jeanie had traveled the universe and was at heaven's doorstep. And she returned in the blink of an eye—just like that! Likewise, in that very same blink of an eye, I was dramatically and forever transformed. I finally realized the true blessings that the Lord had given me, my wife and family and many others. I do not know why the Lord blessed me with such a wonderful, beautiful wife, but I remain thankful beyond words.

Throughout her illness, Jeanie remained stoic and warrior-like. She underwent chemotherapy and a prescription regimen which changed her beautiful outside appearance. Eventually, she decided to push, by will, the Lupus symptoms out and to take no medicine. As a result of her stoicism and will, medication is no longer needed; the Lupus is in remission and she is once again as beautiful outside as she has always been inside.

In that eventful blink, ending in my transformation, it was revealed that, in reality, Jeanie had been placed in my life to give me strength, courage and character—not the other way around. My transformation clarified immediately that without her in my life and without her influence, I would not be the person I am. Her positive influence has allowed me the opportunity to "pay it forward" to others in many ways. It is only because of her that I am me.

It is hard to know what life would have brought my way without Jeanie in it, but I cannot put into words my humble thanks to my Lord, Jesus Christ, for thinking enough of me to purposefully put her into my life and to influence everything I have ever done. He also, very suddenly and without warning, temporarily "took" her from me only to give her back, once assured of my transformation. I remain transformed by death turned into life…by the sudden flight with faceless angels.

Randall R. Sevenish, Esq.

My Story
Andrea Schmook

If in 1973 someone had told me the turn my life was going to take, what would I have done?

I was married and had two children. We lived in Kenai, Alaska, because my husband worked on an oil platform in the Cook Inlet. We bought our own home. It was my dream house. At the time we were buying our home, we discovered that the oil company he worked for owned the subdivision.

There were problems in our marriage, but it wasn't until 1973 that things began building up. By May, our 16-month-old baby had to have double abdominal surgery. A few weeks later, my husband quit his job on the platform and found that he was blacklisted from working in the oil industry. He drove to Anchorage and joined the Laborers' Union. I stayed in Kenai, but drove back and forth to visit him in Anchorage each week.

On one trip to Kenai, I found a letter stating that the oil company was taking back our home since my husband no longer worked for them. By the middle of November, the oil company had taken possession of our home. By the end of November, my doctor told me I had to have major surgery. On the day that I went into the hospital for surgery, my husband fell at work and ruptured a disk in his back.

All of these things happened within a seven-month period as our life collapsed around us. My husband and I didn't have a strong relationship and neither of us knew how to handle these things. We began fighting and blaming each other for what was wrong. I didn't understand the post-traumatic stress he suffered, having served with the Marines in Vietnam. The post-traumatic stress contributed to the relationship problems we were having and he began using drugs and drinking.

One night while sleeping, I heard a sound in my ears like an engine. It began getting louder and louder and I felt myself lifting out of my body. I was above myself looking down at my body. I tried lifting my arms. I tried to scream, but nothing happened. Then I floated into a tunnel of light. As I entered the tunnel I heard a voice say, "You can come or you can stay." I made the decision to stay and floated back into my body. I sat up in bed; fear gnarled my stomach. I was shaking. From that night on, I began to spiral out of control.

I focused so much attention on my husband, fearing that we would divorce, that I had no insight into what was happening to me. The stress was overwhelming and my inner world began to collapse. I lived in fear of another catastrophic event which might further destroy us. I had sleep problems: My heart palpitated, and panic attacks plagued me. My thoughts raced; my thinking was confused and I was suspicious. I couldn't concentrate and I kept looking over my shoulder, expecting some evil to attack me. I sank into depression. I'd flare up into mental and emotional highs. I paced the floor, not sleeping for days. I was paranoid. I heard voices, hallucinated, and was delusional. I believed I was being punished by God, but I didn't understand why I was being punished.

It took from May 1973 until January 13, 1977, a fateful day in my life, when I was out of control—hearing voices, hallucinating, and delusional—that I lost my identify and assumed the identity of the Virgin Mary. I was taken by the Alaska State Police to Alaska Psychiatric Institution. I was diagnosed with acute paranoid schizophrenia. I was told that my life was over and I'd be in and out of the mental hospital the rest of my life. This became a turning point for me. At that moment I decided that I would never go back there. I thought, "I'm going to prove you wrong. I will get better and I'll help other people know that they can too!"

My self-determination grew into a burning desire to get better. I looked for books that told about people overcoming mental illness, but there weren't any. It seemed hopeless, but my drive to find an answer was strong. My sister gave me the book *Think and Grow Rich* and told me, "If you read this and follow the principles in the book, I guarantee you will get better." Curiosity stirred inside me and I read the book. I discovered the secret: "That whatever the mind can conceive and believe it can achieve."

I began to slowly take control of myself and my life; I made new choices. Things that once seemed important were no longer vital. I made a decision not only to survive, but to thrive and grow. I wrote a vision of the life I wanted to live and I read it to myself every night. I wrote affirmations, reading them hundreds of times and practicing the new behaviors that they suggested. The most important thing was changing my thinking through the use of affirmations. As my belief system changed, I changed, and my life changed for the better! The voices, hallucinations, and delusions were gone. I was living the life I was visualizing. I was reaching a potential that I never knew I had. My perspective of God changed to one of a loving God who wanted me to succeed, to heal and to recover my lost life. I learned that because I am, then I can, and ultimately I will change my life for the better!

I'm glad no one told me the turn my life was going to take back in 1973, because I would have missed out on becoming the person I am today—strong, capable, compassionate, loving, spiritual, forgiving, and confident. Now I'm a consultant, trainer, and educator on healing from mental illness and recovery. I'm available for speaking engagements; I write articles. For six years, I was Director of the Office of Consumer Affairs for the State of Illinois, Division of Mental Health. I worked on contract at Alaska Psychiatric Institute where I was a patient. Currently, I'm the Director of Consumer-Directed Services at Anchorage Community Mental Health Center, where once I was a client. I'm president of Peer Properties, an organization providing housing for people who are homeless and mentally ill, and I'm also project manager for Choices, a non-profit organization of recovered people delivering services to others in need.

That is my story; if it can be of service to you, then, it's your story, too.

Andrea Schmook

AWAKENING
Tristan Truscott

"WAKE UP!" This was a common utterance from my teacher's lips. Whether I was practicing martial arts, yoga, dance or simply taking a walk by his side, my Sensei was constantly provoking me to wake up to the present moment—and to stay in it.

Back in the early 1980s I read a book titled *The Way of the Peaceful Warrior* by Dan Millman. After reading his book I became powerfully driven to find my own "Socrates"—the masterful teacher portrayed in the book. Through my searching for such a person, I believe I was lead to my Sensei to receive teachings similar to those of Dan's character in his book.

I met my Sensei in 1989 at a martial arts center. The moment I met him, I knew he was different than any of the other teachers I had trained with or encountered over the years. What the difference was, I could not put my finger on, but when I looked into his penetrating eyes, I knew he held the secret to something very special, and I wanted to know what that was. I wanted to **be** that difference, whatever it was.

After many years of personal growth and waking up to reality I came to understand what that difference was. Simply put, it was the ability to disconnect from the distracting, busy mind and enter a state of higher awareness. The ancient Samurai called this state of awareness "Mushin"—a state of no mind or no ego.

When in a state of Mushin, there are no longer any mental or emotional obstructions such as self judgment, comparison, fear, anger, jealousy or other aspects of the thinking process. It is an experience of being totally present to reality at that moment—similar to what athletes have termed "getting in the zone."

Another wonderful aspect of the Mushin state is the benefit of being completely still within oneself—more still than anything your mind can imagine. Through the practice of Zen meditation, my Sensei tirelessly trained his students to drop the attachment to their ego, to stay awake to the present moment and to enter into stillness.

You see, the process of waking up goes beyond fear-based programming and limiting methods of thinking. In fact, true waking up takes place when you are transported beyond your ego and your true self emerges in a state of higher consciousness.

Gradually, in spite of my ego's self-centered motives, a calm depth of awareness was growing within me. But progress can sometimes be slow. We may get stuck along the way; we need a catalyst. That is what teachers are for; they are there to help speed up our progress.

Often we are not aware of what is holding us back. Simply put, we cannot see where we need to grow. In order for this waking up to actually take place, we have to be challenged to transcend our limited mental and emotional conditioning. This is no easy task. When push comes to shove, the ego's attachments to its limitations, fears and treasured identity will most certainly surface. This is why teachers must know exactly when to serve as catalysts and have a great level of competence in their areas of assistance.

I had no idea of how childish the ego can be when I began training with my Sensei. It is driven by the need to be the center of attention, to be important, to be loved, to be approved of and constantly adulated.

There were many opportunities for personal growth around my Sensei. He used a variety of training environments, exercises and life situations to help us wake up to our true selves. Whenever my ego was exposed for what it really was and its self-important identity was being threatened, well, let's just say it liked to "freak out!"

Here's what happened to me on one occasion with my teacher. I had been working for days on a project for him. He had needed some poems typed for a lecture he was going to give to about 20 students. I was very pleased that he asked me to assist him and my ego was looking forward to impressing him and the other students with its dictation and assisting skills.

I carefully took the dictation, making sure not to add or leave out anything, copied the poems onto a computer, sized them in a nice font that was easy to read and then printed them out for the day of the reading. I went to bed that night anticipating the acknowledgement I would receive on the following day.

The next day I proudly sat by my Sensei's side ready to pass him the perfectly crafted cue cards. However, things didn't go as I planned. As Sensei read the first poem aloud, he began to make disapproving glances in my direction! These facial expressions were soon followed by more strange and quizzical looks, again, directed toward me! During the next poem he began to mark up the papers with a pen. He said he didn't understand why I had changed the poems.

What? Wait just a minute here! My ego started to freak out beneath its "don't look freaked out" mask.

Why was he doing this? I was totally confused. I hadn't made any mistakes. The words were easy to read. In my opinion, no one could have done a more thorough and accurate job. He asked why had I not written them out exactly as he had dictated them? Was I not paying attention? Did I not proofread my work?

As I sat by his side, struggling with my internal reactions, I was faced with a tremendous hurdle and an amazing opportunity. *What do I do? How do I handle this situation? What about my reputation, my need to be approved of, my self-important identity?*

My Sensei continued to read the poems without saying another word to me.

The next few minutes felt like eternity as my mind marched on with its onslaught of drama-filled dialogue: *You look like a fool. Everyone is judging you. They need to know that you really didn't mess this up. Say something. No, don't say anything, that would be disrespectful. Maybe you really did mess this up. No you didn't, he forgot what he said.* My thoughts went on and on.

But then, suddenly something beautiful happened. It was beyond my conscious thought—*everything became still.*

In my internal scrambling for what to do, I remembered that special characteristic I saw in my Sensei: *stillness.* In that moment, without any effort, all of my years of Mushin training kicked in and I was *thrust* into that stillness.

Even though my head was still spinning, inwardly I had found a place where movement didn't exist. Like the eye of a hurricane, I was in the very center where everything was completely still, while my mind was the turbulent wind spinning around.

It was not a shut-down experience. I had not suppressed my feelings or gone into a state of denial. It was very different. My ego had bottomed out. There was nowhere to go, nowhere to hide. There was no need to cover up and no need to be right. I stepped out of my mind and entered into a timeless dimension beyond thinking; a state of awareness beyond defense or courage. All I can say is that it was and continues to be beautiful. It was a freedom unlike anything I had ever experienced before. I no longer felt hurt, judged, less than or better than. I felt I had woken up to my true self.

These moments are often called a *Satori*—a deep awareness—where everything becomes clear. Everything in my life, up until that point, had been preparing me for that particular Satori to take place. Compare this to being like a ripe fruit that's almost ready to fall, but needs a good tug to be released from the tree. If the fruit does not fall from the tree in a timely fashion it could rot right on the branch!

This is what my Sensei had known all along, and this is why he acted as he did. He wasn't trying to be cruel or rude. He played that game with me out of his compassion for me. He saw I was ready to drop my attachment to being important and wanting others to approve of me. He saw an opportunity and he acted as the loving tug that helped set me free from my ego and take me deeper into the Mushin state.

Ultimately, it was up to me to let go. As much as someone may want to help us, we cannot be forced to change or evolve; we must embrace these opportunities, whatever they may be or look like, if we want to be free.

As we were leaving that evening, my Sensei looked at me, as if he were looking right into my soul and asked, "So, did you wake up today?" I looked back into those penetrating, yet loving, eyes and with a joyful smile was able to say, "Yes, today I woke up a little bit more."

Two gentle smiles met in that wakeful moment. I knew that I had finally become that intriguing something, that still presence, that state of Mushin, that I had fallen in love with all those years ago.

Dear Sensei, thank you for this timeless experience. I will never forget all that you have done for me!

Tristan Truscott

Stories Of Transformation

Everything I Needed for Life I Learned in High School Basketball (Well, Almost!)
Donald W. Mills, Ph.D.

We had a great basketball team my senior year in high school under the leadership of an outstanding coach, Chuck Sutherland, who became the coach of the year for the state of Iowa that season. By the time the season ended, I walked away with some valuable lessons that touch me to this day.

Obeying the Rules
Coach Sutherland had a few team policies that set us apart from other teams. He would not tolerate profanity, poor sportsmanship, late nights, absences from practice, or missing school. We were required to wear stocking caps in winter time, take Vitamin C tablets, and go to bed at a decent hour. He made us all keep our hair at a certain length (short!), no long side burns, no beards (me wearing a beard? Right!). We were not allowed to wear wrist bands, head bands, or other kinds of gaudy-looking sportswear. We were the cleanest-cut team in our conference! Perhaps we looked like geeks to our opponents. Indeed, we were sometimes teased, but our record as the best team in the league, by far, put all of that to silence! Coach had his rules for a reason, and that was to make us a winning team. As a consequence, I learned to respect authority and to obey rules, not just for my sake, but for my team. The lesson remains: I can't be successful in my vocation or life in general, if I do not obey the rules.

Cultivating Self-Discipline
The most difficult time of the season was the beginning. Coach put us through some pretty tough early-season practices. By the time these practices were over, I was exhausted. He explained to us the necessity of such vigorous training. In order to be a successful team, we had to be in better condition than our opponents. Games were won, not in the first quarter, but in the fourth quarter, when fatigue would set in. We learned

that the disciplined person, just like a disciplined team, does what needs to be done, when it needs to be done, not just when it is easy or convenient. I came to realize I had to do what I did not want to do (go through agonizing workouts), in order to do what I really wanted to do (be a good basketball player). That's a valuable life lesson. Those who are most successful do things they do not want to do or do not feel like doing in order to accomplish something they have always wanted to do, whatever that might be. All worthwhile endeavors require self-discipline.

Developing Self-Confidence

As the point guard on our team, I was given the responsibility of setting up the plays and getting the ball to the right person. Sensitive by nature, I would really get down on myself whenever I would turn the ball over or make some other glaring blunder. My coach was constantly reminding me to get over it and do it right the next time. Another life lesson learned: If we dwell upon our past failures, they will likely set us up for failure in the present and future. We need to learn from our mistakes and get over them if we are going to live successfully. "Get it right the next time!" is a helpful tip.

Dealing with Pressure

I look back on some of our close games and recall the importance of keeping cool under pressure. In one particular game we were behind by 6 points with 1 minute to go. This was before the 3-point arc, so the picture looked pretty bleak for our team. My fellow guard, Rudy, and I worked together by forcing turnovers, and were able to tie the score with just 10 seconds left. Rudy stole the ball one more time, passed it to me, and I was fouled with 2 seconds remaining. I sunk both free throws and we won the game. There were many games like that in our season, and, as a result of those experiences, I learned to develop a calm center. In our pressure-packed world, life can be tough. Right now, I have never been busier, but I thank God, who has granted me a level of peace and serenity to be able to enjoy my life despite the weight of life's responsibilities.

Handling Disappointment

We lost only two games our entire season, but both of them were very painful. We dropped a game in the state tournament by a margin of 19 points in front of a huge crowd and a statewide TV audience. We played terribly; our opponents played brilliantly. It was our worst game of the season, and the sportscaster was wondering out loud how we ever made it to the tournament in the first place. That stung, especially since we were ranked No. 2 just about all season long. I learned I don't always get what I want and will not win all the time. That's the mature outlook. Dealing with disappointments with the right attitude can build character, especially when we learn from them and can rise above them.

Shunning Overconfidence

I also learned that, while it was necessary to develop self-confidence, an attitude of overconfidence was extremely detrimental. In a few of our close games, and especially the two games we lost, we were overconfident in our ability to defeat our opponent. Since we had won so many consecutive games, we started to feel as though we were unbeatable. By resting on our laurels, by underestimating our opponents, by becoming smug, we were opening ourselves up for failure. I came away with the realization that whenever we face new challenges, we cannot simply rely upon past successes as guarantee of future success, but must give it our best each time.

Enjoying Team Spirit

One particularly enjoyable part of the season was having my closest friends as my teammates. We loved playing together, and so it really did not matter which one of us scored the most points in any given game or who received the most media attention. All of us enjoyed recognition to some degree or other throughout the season and were able to celebrate each other's accomplishments. I have found that so much can be accomplished for good when we can genuinely celebrate the successes of our colleagues!

Learning Good Sportsmanship

Basketball is one of the most competitive sports. Our pride drives us to win at all costs, and sometimes we forget that it is only a game. While we can learn many lessons from sports, the bottom line is our ability to treat everyone, including our opponents and officials, with respect and dignity. I think the same principle holds true in any relationship.

Cherish the Memories

I received a great gift that season, and I think back on it regularly. Those were great days. I don't get to see my teammates very much, but every time we get together for reunions, we enjoy talking about that time. To my basketball pals, Rudy, Brian, Jim, and Dave, and to our great coach, I say, thanks for your friendship; thanks for the memories!

Donald W. Mills, Ph.D.

Tranceform Your Life, Forever!
Marilyn Devonish

*I*s your glass ever half empty like the rest of ours? It's far too early, what on earth are you so cheerful about? I get asked these sorts of questions often. Now don't get me wrong, I'm not a walking Pollyanna! However, I am predisposed to put things into perspective and to be grateful for where I am and what I'm doing.

These days, I wake up in the morning looking forward to what's in store with a sense of excitement and curiosity about how the day will unfold, what I'll learn, and what I'll be able to achieve.

Was I always this way? While I wish I could say I was, I am grateful I wasn't. If there hadn't been dark times and deep, apparently insurmountable lows, I certainly wouldn't be the person that I am today. So how did I, at 32 years of age, turn my life around and get to a place where I could start to live my life with purpose, fulfill my dreams, and create Trance Formations Limited? I fell ill, put on loads of weight, got bad acne for the first time in my life, and went bald (yes, only a couple millimeters of hair left). I gave up work due to a serious lack of energy, embarked on a career change as slight improvements in health were made, found out my partner was having an affair and, within a couple of days, found myself single and without a job.

When I completed my business degree, I specialized in marketing but had always wondered what it would have been like to major in accounting instead, since I enjoyed the subject. It nagged away at me for several years, so I decided to take the plunge, give up my job, and go back to college. It was really hard work, and, because my health was failing, extremely exhausting.

Half-way through the training I decided that I would like to add consulting to my repertoire in accounting. However, because I was inwardly shy, lacking in confidence, and had spent all of my post graduation career "punching below my weight," I didn't think I was good enough to get a "real job" and take the lead.

One day, while discussing an upcoming project with a colleague, I mentioned what I hoped to do when I qualified as an accountant. She mentioned Neuro Linguistic Programming (NLP) as a great way of boosting confidence and self esteem. I'd never heard of it, but after I made some enquiries, I signed up for a course. The rest, as they say, is history.

My biggest worry about completing the NLP course was the classroom contact hours. My energy was incredibly low and I found it difficult to get through a regular day—whereas the course ran from 8 a.m. to 8 p.m. But by the end of the first seven days, I was full of energy. I ran into a friend who asked if I'd been away on holiday because I looked so radiant. That, for me, was confirmation that, after years of searching, I was finally on the right path.

Suddenly I found myself changing from Miss "Oh I wish I could do that," to Miss "When can I start?" I was still me, but a more confident, self-assured, positive and optimistic version. I felt as though I was finally being myself. Challenges became opportunities, failure became feedback, and "I can't" became "I can." I found my voice, and was able to start expressing what was in my heart, rather than the constant fear and worry that had always been in the pit of my stomach.

So how did I do it, and what enabled me to make the instant decision to give up on two years worth of accountancy studies to become a Life Coach, Hypnotherapist, and NLP Trainer? I realized that it was possible to change my long-held values and beliefs if they were no longer working. I realized that life should be a journey. I discovered that I had a powerful ally in my inner mind and learned how to listen to myself—*I* could change and influence my future. Most of all, I started to really appreciate *me*.

My intuition had always been good, but I'd often suppressed, ignored and distrusted it. Even when I knew in my heart that something wasn't working out, if a better and safer alternative wasn't immediately on the horizon, I'd put up with things, bide my time and stick it out.

There was a moment in my NLP Master Practitioner training when a fellow delegate said she couldn't see such a vibrant, bubbly, and energetic person like myself being an accountant, and asked whether I'd considered becoming a Life Coach instead. My automatic response was, "I've invested a lot of time and money in my accountancy training so I am going to complete it, even if it kills me." As the words left my mouth, they made me shiver. I realized why I wanted to be an accountant, and it was for all the wrong reasons. It also suddenly dawned on me that there might be a link between the situation of my life and my health.

When potential clients call for a chat, I share with them some of the simple, but powerful, principles that enabled me to change my mindset and break out of imagined limitations. I will share a couple with you:

1. **You get what you focus on, so focus on what you want.** If you don't want things to go wrong, ask "What do I want instead?" By focusing on the negative aspects of life, you are instructing your mind to focus on the wrong things, and those are the things you will start to draw into your life.

2. **Start seeing failure as feedback.** Ask yourself what you can learn from the situation you are in. Decide what part you played in the scenario, and ask what you are going to do differently next time. You will automatically start building a new strategy and creating new neurological pathways. Should you find yourself in a similar situation in the future, your mind will have a good idea of where to start and what to do.

3. **You either get a result, or you have a reason for not achieving it.**
   Beyond the usual suspects such as lack of time, experience, or
   money, ask yourself what else really stops you from achieving what
   you want. Once you start getting to the core, you will have the
   opportunity to do something about it. If the problem remains in
   the shadows, it will become a silent saboteur in everything you do.

I was someone who was once terrified of public speaking, but I now
train others in public speaking skills and travel the country running
workshops and giving talks on emotional health and well-being. It still
makes me smile when people come up at the end of my workshops and
say, "But it's okay for you, you're a natural." It reminds me that it really
is possible to transform your life—I'm living proof.

Marilyn Devonish

NEVER EVER GIVE UP!
Coral M. Majoor

I have been gifted with many healing capabilities that I have used to heal the sick or hurting in the world around me. I remember one day when I was five-years-old, my pet baby chicken died. My mother brought it to me on a shovel so I could bury it. Instead, I picked it up and placed it between my hands and prayed, "Please God don't let my little chicken die." I rubbed its heart with my hands, and suddenly, it sat up, completely healed and healthy. I looked up and silently thanked God. These healing abilities have allowed me to assist others throughout my life. I have always had an amazing rapport with animals and children.

Eight years ago, I received the most painful phone call from my son. "Mum, it is the worst day of my life. Baby Shane just drowned," he said.

I couldn't believe my ears. My grandson would have been two-years-old in three days. After receiving that horrible news, I made the decision to leave South Australia and let go of everything I owned or knew, to go and be with my son in Queensland. My decision to move meant leaving my beautiful, grown daughter, Bianca, behind with her father. However, she understood my decision and her strength astonished me. "Jace needs you," she told me.

At that time, I was grief stricken, but I was also suffering from physical change and pain as well. I was going through menopause and the effects sometimes stopped me from functioning. I remember one time when I was in my car at an intersection, waiting for a stoplight to turn green. When it did, I suddenly couldn't remember how to put the car in gear! I was panicked. Finally, I was able to pull over to the side of the road and seek assistance from a medical center.

As the side effects of menopause worsened, I tried every type of natural remedy on the market to treat them, and many treatments worked for a little while, but there were some symptoms I could not seem to get rid of. Finally, I met Diana and Roger Beckwith, who introduced me to the products of a company called MiEssence™. It is the world's first extensive range of internationally certified organic make-up, hair, body, oral (probiotic) and skin care company. After using their products for three months, my symptoms were gone. I never suffered from another hot flush again. The products improved my health as well as my appearance, and I began to notice some weight loss and fewer lines and wrinkles around my eyes. I loved the products so much I joined MiEssence™ as a representative and I have never stopped using them since.

During that time, I also had a frozen shoulder that had crippled me for months. I lost the use of my right arm and could not even hold a pen. The doctors told me I had suffered a stroke, but I knew I hadn't. I decided to try BOWEN therapy, and after only one visit I could hold a pen again. The therapy balanced my body. I was so amazed by the results I enrolled in classes to learn how to treat others with this type of therapy. Since I began practicing BOWEN, I have seen amazing things happen. I once saw a five-year-old girl with tonsilitis heal through BOWEN therapy, so much so, she no longer required surgery. I have also seen children with cerebral palsy able to move freely again.

Having learned the healing technique, Reiki (as I am a Reiki Master), along with BOWEN, became a source of great healing after my 11-year-old grandson, Craig, was hit by a car in April 2006. The damage to his body was extensive and he was placed on life support. When I saw him in the hospital with all of the tubes and machines, I couldn't feel his soul anywhere in the room. When I arrived home I looked out over the veranda and saw a magnificent sunset that gave me hope and reminded me to be grateful, even in these hard circumstances.

During that time my darling Mum, many of my family, friends and colleagues prayed that Craig would heal. One day, after praying with a local healing group, I returned to my home and began to meditate. I had a vision of Craig, whose soul was still trapped at the scene of the accident. He was very confused. Through telepathy, I was able to communicate with him and guide his confused soul from the scene of the accident to the hospital room where his body lay. Then, I knew he was safe and going to recover.

Later, I went to his hospital room with my daughter-in-law, Leanne, to visit him. We were told he had been able to move most parts of his body, except for his left arm. Leanne stood on the right side of the bed and I stood on his left side and began to perform Reiki on his arm. Minutes later, his left arm moved. After doing BOWEN, my son moved Craig and his dislocated shoulder went back into place. Through these healing abilities and the prayers of others, I was able to see my grandson achieve a full recovery. Each of the prayers I prayed during that time were answered. Later, Craig told me, "I knew I would be normal!"

I am blessed to be able to do psychic, distance healing (BOWEN included) anywhere in the world. I also teach and educate parents how to choose the sex of their baby. It worked for me: I have my boy (now 32) and my girl (now 25) – oh what a joy! With two new grandchildren, Aiden and Cody.

Through everything my family and I have experienced, I have learned that LOVE and being there for one another are the answers. My abilities may be used for the benefit of all mankind, and in order to use them, I must take action and focus on ways to manifest what I want. I want to heal, instruct and teach others how they, too, may experience these life-changing benefits.

With love and gratitude,

Coral M. Majoor

Symmetry Within: A Personal Story of Healing and Prosperity

Sydeny Bhebe

After countless journeys and wanderings
Through forests, tunnels and blunderings
After many trials and experiments
We return Home to discover and experience
The tremendous Power Within Us
And the Infinite Symmetry in Being Us.

When I think about the way I lived a few years ago, and the way I am now, it is difficult for me to believe the changes. You see, my life was a "right mess." I was drinking daily and heavily, struggling financially despite a thriving business in the hospitality industry, and struggling to complete a Master's degree. Inevitably, I also began to suffer ill-health.

I was born in 1960 in Zimbabwe, a beautiful country in Southern Africa. We were—and are—a Christian family; my father is a church minister, and my mother a teacher. I was blessed with an inquisitive mind, such that I generally excelled in all subjects. However, my main interests were mathematics, physics, astronomy, music and art.

After our country became independent in 1980, I got a wonderful well-paying job with great prospects for promotion, learning opportunities, travel around the world, and recognition. In due course, all these benefits were accorded to me. I also went into business in the hospitality industry, running a bar/restaurant and night club. Unfortunately, I began to drink heavily, such that at one stage I was drinking daily, sleeping late, and eating irregular meals—mainly junk. The money from the business was "rolling in," yet I was struggling to make ends meet.

On the surface my life seemed to be perfect—many people expressed envy of me. But my inner feelings were in turmoil. Because of my hectic lifestyle, I kept postponing exams for my Master's degree in business administration. I spent very little time with my family, justifying to myself that once I made "enough" money I would rest and have much more time for my family. My body started giving warning signs, which I initially ignored. However, the inner restlessness began to grow, and during moments of introspection I realized that my life was unfulfilled. The climax came when I was told that I had high blood pressure. That hit me pretty hard because I was advised to stop what I had hitherto considered to be central to my life—partying and drinking alcohol. At first I tried to ignore the advice, rationalizing that I would reduce, rather than stop, drinking. But my body could no longer tolerate any alcohol. I suppose, as one of my friends joked, "I had used up my allocation."

The drug combination I was taking was effective in normalizing my blood pressure as long as I continued to take them. Unfortunately none of my doctors bothered to tell me about the potential side effects of the drugs, some of which were severe. I experienced queasiness, cold fingers and toes, headaches and other unpleasant symptoms. When I went back to my doctors and explained my symptoms, they prescribed more drugs. At one stage, I was taking 16 tablets a day! Some doctors told me these effects were natural, as I had passed 40 years of age!

Eventually I started my own research, by buying books on health, relaxation, drug interactions, and alternative healing. I also joined a public library, where through unexplainable serendipity I came across Louise Hay's book *You Can Heal Your Life* and Dr. Wayne Dyer's *Pulling Your Own Strings*. I also read other writers such as Theron Q. Dumont and Arthur Koestler. I began to realize that one should not be a passive non-participant in his own healing, leaving it to others.

I took my findings on the side effects of the drugs I was taking to my doctor. I was quite excited, expecting him to be pleased with my initiative. I was somewhat deflated when he gave a lukewarm response, stating that my research was "academic," as all that I had learned was common knowledge! His attitude was that I should leave healing to the professionals even though it involved my body.

Some time later I experienced sudden weight loss, diminished eyesight, frequent urination and severe thirst—the symptoms of diabetes. I was tested and my sugar level was so high that doctors could not believe that I was still conscious. This time I did not panic, because I knew about holistic approaches to healing. A combination of prayer, conventional therapy, holistic healing and natural herbs has resulted in complete alleviation of my negative side effects. I no longer need daily medication for diabetes, and I take only one herbal supplement for my blood pressure.

I have resumed studies for my Master's degree. I am also pursuing a Bachelor's degree in finance and computer management. I have started music lessons, and am composing poems for a book I intend to publish. In short, my life is back on an even keel and I am thankful for the power I received from God to overcome ill-health and an unfulfilling lifestyle.

Every day I acknowledge with gratitude the abundant blessings that God gave me and my family and wish to say that no matter what difficulties one may face, they can be overcome with abiding faith, belief, prayer, meditation, and the support of wonderful people— authors, spiritual guides, and other helpers. This may sound outrageous to some, but these methods can apply even to so-called "incurable illnesses." If one considers that there are many levels of healing, then this Universal Law becomes self-evident.

The key to transformation is you.

Sydeny Bhebe

How Fear Became My Wake Up Call
Shirley McAllister Orf

Fear has always been a thread in my life, yet it was a blessing in disguise when it became my wake-up call. As a child, I found excitement in being scared. I loved horror movies and the adrenaline rush I got from riding a roller coaster. When I was seven, my dad died. Death did not scare me. We went to church every Sunday where we were taught to fear God. In my late teens, I decided God and religion were not for me.

The Federal Reserve
While a Senior at McKinley High School, I worked afternoons at the Federal Reserve Bank of St. Louis. Following graduation in 1966, I was offered a full-time job and worked until 1979 when I took early retirement to go to college. I loved working downtown, I loved my job and the people at The Fed. As Utility Clerk in Safekeeping, I thrived on variety. I learned to think out of the box and lost my fear of change.

Horses
During a trail ride in the mid 1970s, I discovered that, while I loved horses, I was also afraid of them. To conquer that fear, I took riding lessons.

Through my friend Millie Truscott, I met Laura Carpenter, who immediately became my favorite instructor. Millie and I trained on English saddles with Laura's Connemaras (strong, agile Irish ponies). A gentle gelding named Red was my favorite. As an alternative to our fun Saturday morning riding and jumping lessons, sometimes Laura would guide us off-trail around her farm, which was thrilling.

Through Millie, I also met Emily Stickle, who later hired me as a part-time Stable Manager. By that time, I was at ease around horses. In fact, I was in heaven! My favorite horse was a big gelding named Bubba. From their Chesterfield ranch, he and I went on many trail rides at nearby Babler State Park. I loved him as if he were my own and cried the day Emily told me he had to be put down.

Unknown Fears
My unknown fears spiraled out of control in 1987. My thoughts raced, my anxiety was high, and I could not relax or concentrate. Unlike earlier experiences such as this, I did not know how to help myself. I tried to draw on my own strength, but I failed.

Although I never heard voices, I was nevertheless diagnosed with Paranoid Schizophrenia. When the psychiatrist said those words to me, I was devastated. I knew I needed professional help, but I also knew in my heart that I was not crazy. Feeling helpless, hopeless and terrified, finally I submitted to a two-week in-patient care program followed by two years of outpatient care. Mind-altering medication slowed down my thoughts, and I thought that any chance at a normal life was lost.

Angels, Teachers and Therapists
I never feared angels. I believe that unseen help came to me from Archangel Raphael, the angel of healing. By 1990, the energy returned to begin my search for alternative treatments to help me function better. First, I changed my thinking. Second, I asked for higher help. I wondered why I hadn't asked for this help sooner. I was not ready to heal. The most awesome therapists and teachers began to come into my life, and I got better every day.

Part of my in-patient therapy included making arts and crafts. I adopted this as a key to self-care. I had no desire to pursue a degree in art, so I registered for every fun art class I could find instead. Art was therapeutic for the over-active left side of my brain, and a positive outlet for the under-stimulated right side of my brain.

One day in 1991, I heard an interview on local radio about a new business opening for massage therapy, which led me to Laura Kanne. In addition to eliminating the physical pain I felt using acupressure massage, Laura also changed the course of my life by loaning me a book, *You Can Heal Your Life* by Louise Hay. It was my introduction to metaphysics. Little did I know that it would eventually lead me to God. I learned that when I helped one level of my being (mental, physical, emotional or spiritual) I helped them all because they are all connected.

Enneagram

A circuitous path led me to the Maria Center and The Enneagram, an ancient system of personality typing. The Enneagram helped me understand myself. This powerful system revealed my subconscious motivations. During one intense weekend in 1992, I found a startling connection between my birthdate and my Enneagram type. My theory reveals the key which unlocks the Enneagram.

Meanwhile, I continued to receive professional help. I did everything in my power to help myself. I switched from horror movies to comedies. I continued to do more activities that stimulated the right side of my brain. I learned to take responsibility for everything in my life. My mental dysfunction was the manifestation of my out-of-balance brain energy and my spiritual awareness. I learned that I had attracted all of it with my thinking. I learned what was meant by the word "co-create"—do what I can and let God do the rest.

My dysfunction was the manifestation of my out-of-balance brain energy. Much of my current help for anxiety comes in the form of the CDs called Holosync and Paraliminals. Both are easy forms of meditation and quieting of the mind.

Anger, Forgiveness and Letting Go

Throughout most of the 90s I still had issues to deal with, and I was angry. The year that my mother and our black lab, Toby, died was an especially tough year for me. I found a church I liked, which helped me cope. One Sunday at Unity Christ Church, Mark Madsen gave away free tapes of his powerful song, "The Forgiveness Song," later released on CD and MP3.

I was tired of being angry, so I began to work at forgiveness. Forgiving myself and others was not easy or quick. I stimulated as much of my brain as possible by seeing the words of his song, hearing the music and singing along until I was no longer simply singing words. Feelings came alive, as if my heart had suddenly opened. I felt all the feelings and all the grief shut down. As I released my anger, I tore down my resistance to God. I stopped feeling angry, let go, and let God love me.

Life Purposes and Gratitude
Now I know my life's purposes: to express God's love for me through my passions for writing, pottery, animals, art, life, writing and being of service to others.

I feel grateful for everything that has happened in my life. I survived the transformation. Fear was my wake-up call. Without that mountain of fear to climb, I never would have chosen the path which led me to the valley of inner peace. Without all of those experiences, I would have remained living a life of mediocrity, and I would not have become the loving, authentic, creative person that I am today. With God's help and the support of my many friends, family, and my loving husband, Gene, I am now living the life that I love.

Shirley McAllister Orf

Flame on the Heart
Marcos S.R. Ferreira, M.D.

In my life journey, I know that I must be willing to learn, grow, and change every day. Even small things can have a great impact on my life.

My parents were not educated, but they knew the value of education. They began to teach me the importance of learning and being the best I could be when I was very young. Their constant encouragement gave me hope that someday I would be a winner. I believe everyone should strive to be the best they can be.

There is a fire flaming inside our hearts, waiting to be found. How can we find it? I want to share with you what worked for me. I hope that my story will spark your desire to change, too.

I followed the path of education and became a medical doctor, with a post-graduate degree in psychiatry.

In my practice, I saw patients with problems such as depression, bipolar disorder, personality disorder, and so on. I prescribed medication and many of them got better. Unfortunately, others didn't. I became frustrated. I realized that, even though I was a good doctor, dealing with illness and suffering made me very unhappy. I knew, deep inside of my soul, that there was more out there waiting for me.

I decided to look for new activities that embraced health. I took a different course, because I believe that we become what we think. I was becoming depressed myself, from the stress of hearing about the problems, suffering, unhappiness, sadness, and anger of others. I felt like a "magnet" for those who were unhappy. Even in the middle of the street, people would come up to me and tell me about their tragedies. Enough! My goal, during this time was to persevere, to look ahead, and never give up my hope of changing my lifestyle and my daily work. "Someday, somehow, everything is going to be better,"I repeated to myself. Finally that day arrived.

One day I decided to take a course in Integrated Coaching in Curitiba, Brazil. My fear was that it would be one more course among others; more wasted money. But that course changed my life. It turned my flame on. It taught me to take care of people, focusing on health instead of disease, focusing on goals to achieve instead of problems to solve. That course touched my heart. It was eight days of immersion with people from several parts of Brazil. The coach, our professor, was an example of a warm-hearted human being. I realized that my being was lacking humanity. I had the technical knowledge, but lacked compassion and admiration for others. I had a smile on my face, but no gladness in my heart for sharing moments and growing. I had the profession, but not the mission.

At the end of the course, we closed our eyes in meditation. Our coach started talking to our hearts. He told us that we were there not by chance, but that we had a purpose in life; to light other lives. I cried; we hugged each other. I embraced the coach and he looked into my eyes, and said: "This is one of the best moments of my life." And he said quietly from his heart, "Now you know. Your flame is on, the value of life is to light other flames." I've learned to be leader-coach.

For many years I just lived day after day. Is there anyone for whom I really made a difference? I don't think so. Since that moment, I know I can make a difference if I seek to light new flames wherever I am, whatever I'm doing, whoever I'm with.

My goal is to light as many flames I can in my lifetime, to run around the world, passing ahead the flaming torches for a new generation of people who will love to learn, grow and change every single day. Small things, big things—it doesn't matter. Everybody has all the qualities to become a giant. Everybody has the opportunity to wake up. So, the world will see a brotherhood of enlightened people and our example will speak louder than any advice or promise of future peace. It's up to you find your light. Start right now; we need more partners in this journey. Come with us and bring others! There is a secret: We need to receive the light from someone to find our own brilliance. After that, it is your turn to give the little push that is missing and teach the secret to others.

Marcos S.R. Ferreira, M.D.

Having a Purpose and a Gratitude Stone
Namiko Kominami, M.D.

I have heard often that as soon as I distinguished what was so—what was real—I would clear away confusion. As uncertainty clears up, so do the clouds. Even in the face of this knowledge, I find myself unhappy and ineffective from time to time.

One morning I woke up feeling depressed, which I did not like at all. I saw my day as being full of things I had to do that I could not do. In an attempt to do something, I started writing my thoughts. I saw that my thoughts were very negative and I was whining and complaining. I wrote; "Pete hasn't answered me; I am frustrated"; "Steve hasn't responded to my last email"; "My day is not going to work"; I haven't accomplished half what I had planned;" "No amount of programs or books or tapes on success is going to help me." After a few minutes a voice in my head suggested, "Nami, why not rewrite all your complaints as goals?"

I did. Instead of noting that Pete had not returned my call, I wrote, "I want Pete to call today," and so on, until I had 30 goals. Then when I looked at each goal, I saw where I could take the initiative. The next rendition of my 30 items went like this: "Call Pete today to request (this)," or "Do (this) by next Friday." Before I had finished the list, I had called everyone on it and established my next step for projects. By that time, I had awakened to the certainty that my life consisted of real actions to take one step at a time. A shift in my worldview allowed me to leave the shadows and walk into the light full of stamina and joy.

I think the most important tool for me to have that shift in my worldview was living each day with a purpose worthy of my life. I had lived a long time without knowing the difference between my purpose and my goals.

When I was 20, I fell in love with a man 10 years my senior. I stayed with him through many trials and dramas. I discovered he had girlfriends other than me. Then he married someone else and then called and asked me to wait for him to get a divorce. Finally, after 12 years of turmoil, we married. The first year was blissful! But after that our daily life consisted mostly of arguments. If I had only known then the importance of living on purpose—"I intend to create a marriage that is the foundation of safety and love to nurture both my husband and me and to support our going out into society to work and contribute." With a purpose for our relationship, we might have ignored our differences. Without a high perspective, I allowed insignificant things to take center stage, which eventually led to divorce. Unfortunately, I repeated that scenario again before I finally woke up.

Now, at the beginning of each year I ask myself what is the meaning of my life? What do I stand for? What is my mission, my cause for existence? Then I create a purpose, and live with it for a while. I change it until it calls to me, is just right for me, and inspires and empowers me. I know also that setting a purpose before doing anything works in my subconscious mind to direct my actions and thoughts. This is the most amazing part of having a purpose. My ability to act to make my whining and complaints into a doable list of actions is one such example.

I am committed to these ideals:

- My purpose is to save humanity.
- Who I am is the light.
- My mission is to bring about a spiritual renaissance in Japan by 2031.
- My purpose is to save myself, to develop spiritually, and to relate to all beings with unconditional love and compassion.
- I intend to write, develop programs, and lead seminars to help the people in Japan develop spiritually.

Besides having a purpose worth living for, self-awareness allows me to observe what I am being, doing, and having at any given moment. I practice noticing what I am seeing while driving, walking, eating, etc. I do it until I realize that my mind has wandered. At first I berated myself for losing concentration, but I continued my practice. Soon I stopped resisting and struggling. Observing became second nature. The most wonderful benefit I discovered was that whatever I observed, I was able to accept, transcend, and include.

Another key that contributed to my waking up was my willingness to see the truth. I learned to differentiate reality from my own story, judgments, evaluations, and preferences. Then I became clear about what I wanted and patient enough to study my negativity. Even if things were not turning out the way I had expected or wanted, I persisted instead of interpreting the situation as failure. Now I respond by changing my attitude. I keep clarifying my next step and taking it, trusting that I will achieve what I want for the good of all.

My strongest antidote to negativity is to practice being grateful for whatever results I get. My habit of gratitude attracts success, fulfillment, and satisfaction. Still, I notice my tendency to negativity as though it were in the air I breathe. What sort of forces do I attract from being negative? Dr. Hawkins says that the antidote for negativity is gratitude. I now carry a small stone of gratitude in my pocket. Whenever I get negative, depressed, or critical of myself or others, I touch it and offer thanks for whatever I am facing.

I practice acknowledging unpleasant and unwanted emotions and then acting appropriately to fulfill my purpose. I strive to act lovingly, thoughtfully, and compassionately toward myself and others. Now, even when I feel afraid, I choose confidence and self-assurance. Dark moods still descend from time to time. I honor them for a moment for what they can teach me. Then I renew my commitments. My purpose and goals wake me up and guide me to live the life I love.

Namiko Kominami, M.D.

THE LENS OF YOUR LIFE
Linda Y. Kalnins M.D.

One day, an elderly man was complaining of blurred vision, so he went to see his ophthalmologist.

"You have a cataract," the doctor said. "What does that mean?" said the patient.

"It means your vision is being blocked; light can't enter the eye so you won't see clearly," replied the doctor.

"Can it be fixed?" asked the patient. "Yes," said the doctor, "I can remove the cloudy lens and replace it with a new lens. The power will be specific to your eye and you will be able to see clearly again."

"So I will get my vision back?" said the patient. "Only if you would like," said the doctor.

We all can create and manifest our own unique vision of our lives, lives we love, filled with meaning and purpose. Manifesting this vision starts with belief in self.

Believe in Yourself
"Believe in yourself," my parents used to say. Facing exile to Siberia during World War II, my parents fled to the United States. They were well-educated, cultured, and well-to-do. They had had a high standard of living. They lost it all. Despite this, my parents recreated successful lives. Something about their thinking worked! We lived in a wealthy suburb of metropolitan New York and I graduated from a prestigious private high school. Although my grades and test results were excellent, my guidance counselor advised me not to apply to Ivy League universities—so I didn't. Unfortunately that was just the advisor's opinion. I placed out of all my freshman requirements at an excellent

university, even as a science major. I had learned my lesson—believe in yourself! Planning to go to medical school, I approached the dean with my idea of graduating in three years.

"You can't do that!" he replied. "Why? I asked. "It's just not done here!" he replied.

After much persistence, I graduated in three years and applied to medical school. (The university subsequently changed the bylaws to require four years of attendance.) The year I applied there were over 9,000 applicants for roughly 200 positions at the medical school that was my first choice. All I heard was, "Believe in yourself." I was accepted.

Hard Work/ Sacrifice
"You can build a new life any time with good old-fashioned hard work," said my dad.

"You can lose everything, but you can never lose your education and your freedom of thought," my mom would say.

I sacrificed, put in my time, and applied for the most sought-after residency at the time: eye surgery. I became one of the few women who made up only 2% of existing eye surgeons. I sacrificed much of my twenties, my sleep and free time, but ultimately I knew that putting in my time would lead me to the life I would love. I established my own practice in the early 1990s, just as the consultants were predicting the demise of the solo practitioner. "It can't be done," they said. My peers agreed and all joined groups, but I had learned my lesson. I hung out my shingle and began the life I loved.

I learned a lot from my patients over the years, but I have also learned by listening to and observing people in general. We all can do that if we simply pay attention.

Have Courage/Persevere
The businessman with endless diabetic eye disease perseveres with his treatments and demonstrates the courage to face blindness. He overcomes resistance and accepts his situation while simultaneously working to change it.

Create/The Power of You
The best-selling elderly author who recently lost all vision in one eye from glaucoma keeps churning out books on his computer because life is about creation and expressing oneself.

Change Your Path/Life Is a Journey
Every few years, when this man comes in for an exam, he has a new career. The restaurant owner, turned engineer, turned teacher, who is successful at everything he tries shows us that our purpose can change. Sometimes in life you need to change course to be true to yourself. Too many people just stick with what they know, even if it is no longer working for them. Life is a journey, not a destination.

Limiting Beliefs
A young man presents with eye trauma and seemingly no hope for vision. He insists he will see again. Miraculously, after surgery he sees 20/20. Never say, "Never."

Follow Your Bliss
The fifty-two-year-old mom with blurred vision from radiation treatments has been given less than a year to live. She prods us. Life is short. If your days were numbered, what would you do? Be happy.

Be Silent
The nun, who can no longer read because of macular degeneration, reminds us to be still and meditate. Silence cultivates inner peace, creativity, and great ideas.

Live in the Now

The endless array of geriatric patients who repeatedly harp, "Don't get old!" remind us to live in the moment. Do not postpone happiness.

Give Back

The healthcare worker who returns from Africa with a blinding eye infection says it is still worth it to help the sick, uneducated, and indigent in developing nations. She reminds us that we are part of a larger whole.

I have learned a lot listening to my patients. Although personal clinical care has been meaningful, I am now prepared to help people on a greater scale. I have decided I can best do this by writing and I am spending more time authoring articles, newsletters and books. This is my way of creating, teaching and ultimately helping society. My path has changed and I am following my bliss. I still apply all of the principles that I have learned in my life and I am still listening and observing. You can do this too.

As the patient learned before his cataract surgery, wherever the focus is, the vision will be clearest. By replacing the lens, we can put things in focus wherever we want. Our life purpose is the same. The lens of perception is whatever we want it to be. We choose our focus, and we choose our purpose. Life is what we make it.

Pick your purpose and live it: Live the Life You Love!

Linda Y. Kalnins M.D.

LEARNING TO BE A CONSCIOUS CREATOR
Constance Haldaman

S ome of us seem to take longer to learn certain truths. I was one of
those people.

My spiritual quest began around the age of 11, but if you saw a graph
of my progress it would look like the Rocky Mountains—high peaks
and deep valleys. I used to beat myself up for being that way, but I
have finally learned to love myself enough to realize that this was my
path. I became the person I am today because of the choices I made.
Before I realized that I was the creator of my own life and, therefore,
responsible for everything in it, I unconsciously created a lot of
unnecessary obstacles. Yet, in spite of my ignorance of the natural laws
of the universe, I had enough desire and drive to accomplish much,
even though I fell short of the fame and fortune I dreamed of as a child.

At the age of 13, I was under contract to a major record label as a
singer/songwriter. I taught piano and voice lessons, sang in nightclubs
and musicals, and later on, had a moderately successful career as an
opera singer. After that, I worked in television with my former husband,
producing, writing and hosting nationally syndicated shows for cable
television. I composed award-winning music for commercials, raised
horses, and sold them as far away as New Zealand, helping to preserve a
breed that was on the verge of being lost. Still, I was an unconscious
creator who never had enough belief in myself or my abilities.

My real transformation began when, after more than 20 years of marriage,
I found myself alone without any income except for the occasional sale of
horses. I was 58 when my husband left and I was very scared. I had no
idea how I would earn enough money to support myself. I felt lost. That
is when my real spiritual and personal growth began, and it has been a
steady upward climb ever since. Still, it took me quite a while to figure
out what I wanted to do with the rest of my life.

Somehow I ended up at one of Bob Proctor's seminars and took advantage of a special offer for personal coaching in a program called "Lead the Field." That program literally saved my life. I began to have creative ideas again and dream about the kind of future I wanted to create. Out of those ideas emerged the desire to become a life coach and someday have my own retreat that would involve healing with horses, along with other modalities.

Two years later, I had become a certified life coach and began working with clients. I only had a few and was trying to learn how to market myself. I knew I was a good coach and had much to offer, but the marketing concepts scared me. Therefore, my progress was slower than I would have liked.

In the spring of 2004, I met a wonderful man and became engaged a few months later. We bought a home in the beautiful Colorado resort town where I lived and moved in together in October of that year. A wedding was planned for December and life was wonderful in every way. The future promised to fulfill every dream.

But it was not to be. Within a month, I was diagnosed with breast cancer. Just after Thanksgiving, my fiancée was in a hospice dying from a melanoma that had metastasized throughout his body. His son and daughter chose to put him in a hospice that was over three hours away and, since I was undergoing chemotherapy, I was only able to see him a few times before his death. I was devastated. I wondered why I had created these experiences for myself, but I also knew that I could make the choice to use them as an opportunity for growth.

Two months later, I learned my fiancée's adult children had taken half our home and a small insurance policy that had been left to me. Now, I really began to ask, "What in the world is going on and why all this is happening all at once?" But still I trusted the process.

Suddenly, I had a very adverse reaction to the second course of chemo and made the decision to undergo a mastectomy and reconstruction. I realized that I needed some help to handle everything I was experiencing, and once again I hired a coach who was also a medical intuitive. Working with her helped me stay on course and allowed me to gain more clarity about both my situation and the future I still wished to create. There were many moments of joy and bliss during this most difficult time, and I know that it was because of the positive attitude I worked so hard to maintain. My friends and I even laughed about the soap opera-like life I was living. I still do not know why I experienced so many challenging events in such a short period of time; perhaps I never will. Clearly, I learned that it is not about what happens in our lives, but how we decide to feel about it. I knew that I had drawn these "opportunities" to myself for a reason and it was up to me to make the most of things. I was also given the opportunity to work on forgiving those who had wronged me, and I have to admit it wasn't easy.

It has been almost two years since the mastectomy and I am still cancer free. Everything has been resolved with my fiancée's children and I have blessed them and let them go. I recently made the life-changing decision to relocate to another Colorado town, where I knew not a soul except for my real estate agent. It took a lot of courage to leave the town where I had so many good friends and such a good support system, but I felt that it was time to get out of the cold and live in an area that would provide more opportunities. I have started coaching again, and find myself attracting a lot of people who have physical challenges. It is gratifying to be able to use the wisdom that I have gained to help my clients see the spiritual, physical and emotional aspects of their circumstances and guide them to the understanding that these so-called "negative" events in our lives can be wonderful opportunities for growth. I am currently working toward certification as a health coach to add to my other certifications.

So, here's what I know: My purpose in life is not to *do* any particular thing, but rather to remember who and what I am and to live every day striving to attain that highest vision of myself. Out of my being comes the passion and courage to do the work that fulfills me and lets my light shine to show others the way to their highest vision.

Constance Haldaman

In the Arms of a Loving Universe
Elke Keil

It was July 10, 1997. I stood over my mother's hospice bed and told her I loved her. I asked her if she could see the light, her long departed friend, Billy, and her father. "Please go with them if they are reaching for you," I told her. They called me the next morning to tell me she had passed on.

My mom always worried that she would pass on at the same age her father had. I once told a friend my mother would never live to see her 66th birthday. She was 65 when the doctors misdiagnosed her with lung cancer. My dad couldn't imagine life without my mom and willed himself to death three years later. I watched in horror as my stepsister, a woman we had not seen or heard from in 20 years, appeared on the scene and began searching through all of my parent's belongings for their will. She claimed to be the executor of their estate, but I knew through a message I received from my parents that I was to fulfill that role. It was a traumatic experience, but it showed me I could communicate with my parents in the afterlife. Between the years 2000 and 2001, many people who were close to me died, and this ability to communicate with them helped me get through.

I was born and raised in Germany by my grandparents until the age of 14. Then I moved to the United States to live with my mother and stepfather. Reincarnation and life after death were two beliefs which I acquired early in life. Throughout my life, I had taken my troubles and woes to God and to the people in my life who had passed on.

When I first came to the United States, the loneliness and fear I experienced were terrifying. I could not read, write or speak English, and the transition was very hard—especially since my mother and stepfather were virtual strangers to me. I often thought I must have done something really wrong in a previous life for God to take me away from all the people I knew and loved.

I believe that God helps those who help themselves, so after graduating from high school, I began working as a bookkeeper. I moved out of the house and married, but my marriage was troubled. Over the next few years, I became a mother and the co-owner of several businesses. After my divorce, I was a single mother and business owner. I now work as the controller of a company and as a part-time hypnotherapist and Life Coach. I will soon be a grandma and a graduate of Huntington Pacific University with a PhD in Hypnotherapy.

The countless struggles I have experienced throughout my life have been a great source of comfort to me. I know my parents and other loved ones who have passed on are watching over me, and I can communicate with them. I attribute my good fortune and health to having lived a life of peace, compassion, care, integrity and honesty. I live by the standards of the Golden Rule. When I was not in harmony with my Creator or the earth, I could tell, because I would become sick or challenged in my business and personal life. The forces of the universe presented me with many opportunities for personal growth and understanding, through years of personal and financial woes as well as several injuries that allowed me to learn to heal myself.

I find living my life passionately and with purpose, to be exhilarating. I have created the acronym WATCH (watching my Words, Actions, Thoughts, Character and Habits) to assist me in my work and day-to-day life. As a spiritual life coach, I enjoy assisting others uncover deep-seated limitations that keep them from being their best and living the life of their dreams.

A lifetime of passion and purpose surrounds you; live it fully, for that is your obligation to Him, and those who brought you to life in the first place.

Elke Keil

CREATIVE DISCONTENT: A PATH TO TRANSFORMATION
Dan Selene

People often think of discontent as a negative force but I have found it to be a positive guide. Combined with persistence, it is a key to personal growth and transformation. It helped me transform my life.

I always valued education and was excited to become a teacher. The first several years were very fulfilling but then there was a feeling of discontent. It started out as a whisper...a feeling that, for me, there was something else I was supposed to be doing in life. As time went by, it became stronger until it couldn't be ignored. Looking back, that discontent was a blessing, a message from a place within that new possibilities were calling and an exciting adventure was about to begin.

At the tipping point, I didn't know what I wanted. So I just stopped what I was doing and chose traveling as a means of discovery. I had traveled quite extensively throughout Europe earlier in life, and was quite content with a 20-pound backpack for an overland trip across Turkey, Afghanistan, Iran, Pakistan and India. Throughout the trip I kept hearing about a legendary town in India called Rishikesh in the foothills of the Himalayas. This sounded like the place for me as I was definitely on a mission of self-discovery. I really wanted to find out what had been driving me to change my life.

Fortunately, Rishikesh more than lived up to its reputation. It was a very exotic place with the Ganges River flowing through it, monkeys and parrots in the trees and ancient paths crisscrossing the town. After a few weeks of exploring various ashrams and the caves where the Sadhus "holy men" lived by the river, I discovered a book by Jiddu Krishnamurti. In it he used a term, "creative discontent." He said it was the kind of discontent that brings about change and that it was a good thing to feel it and to follow it. He believed that everyone had an inner voice that provided true guidance for that person. Our job is to clear away the psychic debris and listen. It is not thought, which is conditioning, but rather a pure source impulse. We may call it a "gut feeling."

Then I understood the purpose of the discontent that had driven me to Rishikesh. It was leading the way to change by teaching me to trust my inner guidance. The trip was a faith builder. It resulted in a powerful insight that was going to be absolutely necessary for future transformations.

A few years later, I was in Southern California teaching at a progressive private school with a holistic perspective on education. That was a major transition but there was more to come. I thought I had reached my potential. From the point of view of my background and training, I was doing something that was very fulfilling.

But again I felt that sense of "creative discontent." After my last experience, I realized that I had to honor that feeling. Following the advice of Krishnamurti, I sought to get clear on what I wanted. I began to visualize being an entrepreneur and having a lifestyle business that would encompass all of my interests.

After a 10-year career in education, I was 33-years-old and setting out to completely transform myself into an entrepreneur. I worked at part time and full time jobs in business as I read all the books I could find on the subject of personal growth and transformation with an emphasis on "right livelihood" and career. Although things were going well in other areas of life, I just wasn't making progress toward my goal. I was having doubts. Due to dwindling finances, I needed a more substantial job. Finally, I found a position in a financial services firm, but it was a business culture that was anything but "socially conscious." It was there that I decided I had to get into a business that considered more than profitability—a business that would be a beneficial presence for society. I stayed with the company for a year and then moved back to southern

California to a similar firm.

It had now been almost four long years of working with the principles. I had no outward signs of progress. I was full of inner doubts, questioning my faith, and on the edge of despair.

Once I hit a bottom of unhappiness and my deepest discontent, I just had to let go and find something—anything—else to do. I gave two weeks notice for my job and I just let go. It was a classic "let go and let God" moment with the accompanying mixture of relief, peace and freedom. I went all the way to the end of my rope, and gave up on my vision of success. I thought the feeling would be different. I was approaching my late thirties and was no closer to my dream (I thought) than I had been 4 years earlier.

Then I learned, first hand, the truths I had learned from some of my favorite authors - Napoleon Hill, Bob Proctor, James Allen, David Bohm and Earnest Holmes. When I completely let go, I had no answers to the many issues that were facing me, including the basics of paying bills and finding a new place to live. There was a feeling of having come through a long tunnel of trials and tribulations and that had taken all the energy so there was nothing left. It was just about being empty and seeing what would develop—I think some call it "allowing." The first thing I did was to take a trip to Northern California for some healing and rejuvenation.

One afternoon, I went to a well-stocked local record store and was drawn to two records in the "ambient" music section. I had just discovered this emerging style of music. It seemed there was a shift going on in the music industry as the acoustic instrumental sound had caught on. There was new electronic music from Europe, Japan and Canada as well.

Perhaps because the previous four years had left me depleted and mentally exhausted, the soothing introspective music had a magnetic effect. I absorbed the music over the next few weeks. At one point, I remember sensing an inner awareness that this music was to be a significant part of my future. When I got back home, I had a new direction and felt that I had plugged into a new energy.

Within a month, two amazing things happened. I received a call early one morning offering the ideal part time job. That enabled me to follow my heart because finances were secure. I felt I was living a dream. Then I discovered a college radio program with the best repertoire of the new ambient music from all over the world. I contacted the program director and discovered that his dream was to have the program syndicated nationally. I decided to help, and a few months later our first investor appeared and we were on our way. Six months later, we had our program together and our next partner appeared. He was established in the entertainment industry and suggested that we create a record label as well. After another year of research and development, including lining up distribution and signing our first artist, we were ready to begin.

We incorporated on my 39th birthday and I was very thankful for persistence and in a strange way for all the difficult experiences of the previous 6 years.

Still, that was just a beginning and it took another 4 years before we had our first profitable year. It was challenging but it always seemed to have some sort of blessing and sense of destiny.

A dozen years after we started we were acquired by one of the major record labels. All together, we created 250 albums and had retail sales of $150 million. We created a company which, by all definitions, was my "right livelihood." I was very thankful for the "creative discontent" which had led the way.

When I look back on what I learned through the transformation of my career, the lessons are very familiar. We have all read the words again and again. Fortunately, they are true – "It's never too late," "Don't settle for less," "Never give up."

Dan Selene

THE MIND SIDE OF WEIGHT LOSS: GROW THE MIND TO SHRINK THE BODY
Shane J. James

It Starts With The Mind

Getting in shape, eating healthy, exercising, and choosing good behavior are more internal processes than external ones. When we get the internal stuff working right, the external change is merely a positive by-product. Once we get the internal stuff right, the weight will start to come off externally: If we don't, it is a lot easier to "yo-yo diet." If you're looking for lasting change, it starts in the mind.

Mission Statement

A well-written mission statement gives you direction. Then you can plan to succeed. What is the end result you want? You have to be specific. How many pounds do you want to drop? For example: My purpose is to be at my ideal healthy weight of 150 pounds within 4 months. I plan on accomplishing this goal by listening to "Weight Loss and the Mind" podcasts, doing one hour of exercise per day and following healthy eating plans. I post this plan where I can see it everyday.

Believe You Can

Belief can be the most powerful force for creating a rewarding life. When you believe you can do something, you literally put yourself into a state of it being true. On the other hand, beliefs that limit your thoughts and actions are detrimental to your ability to achieve your ideal, healthy weight. Handled effectively, belief can be the most powerful force in helping create ever-lasting change in your weight. How much do you believe in yourself?

Affirmations Do Change Weight

When you use affirmations, you influence the thoughts that occur in your mind. Your affirmations must all be stated in the positive. We feel much more motivated to accomplish a positive outcome rather than a negative. For example: If you want to achieve your ideal weight you wouldn't say, "I am not going to gain any more weight." The mind will have trouble picking up the word "not" in that statement and will only hear the word "gain." Always state your affirmations in a positive way.

Healthy Self Esteem

Self-esteem affects all areas of your life. What you do, how you do it, how you treat yourself and others, and how much you enjoy life are all affected by your level of self-esteem. If you have low self-esteem you're unlikely to be as motivated to take care of yourself physically, mentally and emotionally as someone who has higher self-esteem; and that means weight control will be more difficult for you. How much a person likes, accepts and respects himself overall sums up self-esteem. Build your self-esteem and watch the inches melt away.

Everyday Positive Emotions

The pictures you run in your mind will create positive or negative emotions. If you picture yourself failing and overweight, you will enter into a state of depression and frustration. If you picture yourself achieving your ideal, healthy weight you will live in a state of joy and happiness. If you run positive, internal representations, you can put yourself into positive states anytime you choose. That's personal power.

Visualize Yourself To Success

Relax deeply and see your desired outcome. The more frequently you visualize a clear mental picture of yourself achieving your ideal, healthy weight the better results you will actually achieve. The longer you can hold a mental picture the more deeply it will be impressed into your unconscious mind, and the more rapidly you will make the change. There is a direct relationship between how clearly you can see your desired outcome in your mind and how quickly you will achieve your outcome.

Action Steps

What are three actions that you could take right now to help change your weight? Go do them now; there's power in momentum. Don't wait until tomorrow.

Everyday, commit to getting up a little bit earlier and plan your days in advance. Plan your meals in advance and take some time to think about your weight goals and how you're going to achieve them. There is power in planning.

Your mind has the power to transform your goals into reality. You may find that these mental habits will not only shrink your weight problem, but will reduce life's tensions, tests and terrors, too.

You have the power.

Shane J. James

The Big Mistake
Maxwell Synsvoll, D.C.

It began as a big mistake. I had spent the better part of my life doing it. I reached out in every direction looking for it and it took 27 years and a major tragedy to find it.

I started out like most Midwestern kids with a phenomenal family and lots of love, but something was wrong. Nobody was aware of it, it was just the way things were. As I grew up, I was sick more often than most of the kids around me. Off to the doctor we would go; they'd give me a shot or a pill and we would be on our way. I loved the doctors so much I wanted to be one. The doctors liked me because I could tell them what drug I needed based on my symptoms. They were amazed at my accuracy—at least so they told me. Years later, my life took a strange twist.

In the summer of 1989, I had a job that required a lot of bending and twisting. At 2:00 one morning, I heard a pop as I bent to pick up a package and felt a stabbing sensation in my lower back. I went to see one of my doctors.

"Take these pills and rotate your back under the hot shower," he told me. "You will get better."

But I did not get better. I got worse, a lot worse. Standing was agonizing. Sitting was agonizing. I went back to the doctors. "Take this pill and it will get better," they told me. "Maybe you should see a surgeon," they later suggested.

My health problems worsened; I was not breathing well, My asthma was getting worse, my energy was low, and my hands were going numb. I was angry. "Why am I getting sicker?" I wondered. Soon, I could not get out of bed or tie my shoes without help. My asthma inhaler was becoming my constant ally. One day, my grandfather told me to try going to a chiropractor. I was ready for anything that might help, so I decided to take his advice.

I went to our family doctor and asked him what he thought. "No!" he said. "That will make you worse! It will be a big mistake!"

"But I'm already getting worse!" I said. Later that day I went to see a chiropractor. There, something happened that changed my life.

The chiropractor examined me, took some x-rays and adjusted my spine. He explained to me that my body contained everything that was necessary for my body to heal. He said that as long as the body is allowed to heal, it will. All he needed to do was remove the interference that was occurring in my spine. This sounded strange to me, but as he worked on my spine, my asthma symptoms went away, my energy returned and the feeling came back into my hands. From that day forward I stopped taking medications. I could walk again without pain.

I was healed and transformed, so much so I decided to become a chiropractor myself. Eleven years later I opened my own practice. That same week, a little boy with blonde hair, blue eyes and pop-bottle-thick glasses was brought in to see me. Over the previous year and a half he had been hospitalized 16 times. His mother said her little boy had been sick since his first week of life with colds, colic, asthma, fatigue, and restlessness. He wanted to be held all the time, he was taking nine different medications, and he had recently begun having seizures and his eyes were crossing.

"Can you help him?" his mother asked. I was about to pass on to him the same big mistake that was passed on to me. I examined him, took some x-rays, and inquired about his birth.

"Were there any forceps used?" I asked.

"Yes," she answered.

"So this was not a gentle delivery?" I asked.

" "No!" she said.

I located a bone at the base of the boy's skull that was twisted out of place and putting pressure on one of the major nerve centers in his body. I explained to the family what I had found and we began the simple and gentle process of removing the pressure.

Within a week, this little boy stopped having seizures and began breathing properly, his eyes even started to uncross and he began putting on weight. His mother asked me what she should do about the nine different medications he had been taking. I told her to ask his pediatrician, and when she did, she was told she was making a big mistake: nothing in the treatment I was giving the boy was proven. She wanted to know why her little boy had not been getting better, and the doctor had no answers to give her. The pediatrician was suffering from the same problem I had suffered from as a little boy. Do you want to know what it was? It was the mistaken and misguided belief that the answers to our problems are somewhere outside of us. It is the false notion that a drug is the answer to any of our troubles. This is a hard one for most people to understand because we are trained to believe that the answer is outside of us, and anyone who tries to teach people that they are incredible healers with the ability to do amazing things is labeled as "crazy." In that case, I like being crazy.

I did not and do not claim to have cured that little boy. What I did do was allow his body to take care of itself by giving it the opportunity to do so.

What started out as a big mistake has turned into the opportunity of a lifetime. I am now asked to speak to and treat people from all over the world and see incredible miracles occur on a daily basis. None of this would have been possible if I had not decided to accept responsibility for my own health and begin looking on the inside for the answers to life's questions. This was the key to opening the door that allowed me to transform and live the life I love.

Maxwell Synsvoll, D.C.

THE ULTIMATE MACHINE
David Alden

I would like to begin by telling you about the most powerful technology known to man. This technology enables you to live the life of your dreams, to have unlimited prosperity, to have the ideal romantic relationship and to be in peak health.

You may wonder how you could obtain such an awesome device. Perhaps you have wondered how to achieve these idealized states of existence. I will share with you how I have utilized this advanced technology known to enhance every area of my own life.

Before I was aware of this great mystery, I found myself alone after a failed marriage and separated from the family and home I loved. I was in despair; it was hard to see beyond the rug being pulled out from underneath me. I was unemployed at the time. I cried every day for a week in my sorry state, but then an amazing thing happened.

I made a decision that changed everything. I chose to shift my thinking and to see that I had been given a great gift. I understood for the first time in many years I was free to become who I was born to be. I had no one demanding I be a certain way—that I fit into a mold and conform to rigid standards. I chose at that moment to accept this gift and move forward with my life as I chose to live it. From that moment on, my life has been a journey of joy, peace, love and deep satisfaction. I now travel the world to help people like you to achieve their dreams. I live in a beautiful home, am married to the woman of my dreams and have a wonderful, loving family.

I think it is appropriate to share with you the name of the technology I have utilized to achieve my dreams. It is greater than the most advanced computer. It is your own mind. The human mind is far more powerful than most people realize or understand. Our Creator, God, Source, or whatever title you may call this Infinite Being, has equipped us with everything we need to accomplish anything we choose. There are no limits, except those we decide for ourselves.

To explain the limitations we place upon ourselves, think about the last time you said yourself, "I can't do that," or "There is no way I could have (fill in the blank)." Each time you think those thoughts, you send a powerful message to the universe, which responds by shaping and forming your experiences to match what you have instructed it to create for you.

You see, each of us create our own reality. The Bible says we are special and different from the other creatures inhabiting the Earth. God/Source/Creator, has given us the gift of being a co-creator. Think about this for a moment and understand what it means: You have the power of your Creator to manifest anything you desire. For me, this is accomplished through having a direct connection to the God Source. We have an unbroken connection to the ultimate creation energy. I have come to know this connection as my Higher Self, or my Infinite Self. The words you choose to use identify this part of yourself are not as important as realizing that who, or what you are is far greater and more powerful than you may have previously realized.

If we focus our awareness on what we desire and make this experience as real as possible to all of our senses, the process begins to work. The unconscious mind does not distinguish between what is physically around us (what people call reality) and what is the reality in our mind, or imagination.

It is not a difficult thing. It all comes down to our thoughts. Our thoughts are the seeds of our future reality. Every thought is a lightning spark that adds to the previous lightning spark, and together these solidify and become the world we see around us. Pay attention to your thoughts. You may ask yourself, "Are my current thoughts empowering me? Do my current thoughts make me feel connected to the Divine and filled with joy, love, peace, harmony and balance?" As we do this more often, the vibration, or speed at which we communicate and co-create, increases. This causes us to be even more powerfully linked to our Higher Self—that part of us that is, always was, and will always be— one with the God Source. We have everything within ourselves that we need to manifest Heaven right here on Earth. It all comes down to thoughts, feelings, and then, taking the actions that we are guided to take.

When we are always coming from our Higher Self, then life flows from one joy to another because we are in perfect sync with the divine plan for our life. This is the true meaning behind what religion refers to as "God's plan for your life."

There are challenges every day. Being human is a tough assignment, but we are never given a challenge too great to rise above and emerge victorious. I know you can do all of this and more. Know that you are never truly alone. All you need to do is ask the universe for whatever you desire. Know that you have a right to everything in life that you choose. I am excited about what the future holds for you. Walk with courage, have a compassionate heart and allow love to flow freely through you out to the world.

It was my honor to relay these messages to you. I hope they have helped and inspired you. This was an introduction to these principles of co-creating your world. More in-depth information is provided in the courses I offer.

David Alden

STORIES OF TRANSFORMATION

TRANSFORMATION
Steven E

Life is always changing. No matter what else may happen, you can count on change. For many, change is quite stressful. One of the most stressful of all changes is finding a new career. Perhaps you've been working just to survive and work has become boring and dull. If you are currently in a job you do not like, take time to work on what you enjoy, and set a timetable for making a change; be patient with yourself. You know there has to be something better out there for you, but what?

I suggest you reach deep into your soul and find the power to transform; sit quietly and think of what you like to do; things that brighten your day and make you smile; those things you would gladly do not for money, but for pure enjoyment. The answer is simple. Transformation lies within each and every one of us.

Begin finding a path to freedom in your employment. Be sure to have as many options as possible, and develop other income-producing ideas. This will grant you flexibility and self-empowerment. Assess your talents and gifts. Find out what you really enjoy and what you do exceptionally well. Learn what they are and develop your inner gifts.

Once you have an idea of what you would like to do in life, write it down. Each morning, meditate or pray on the things you want. Feel and see what you want, see and feel yourself already having it. I believe you can do and can be whatever you desire in life, if only you believe— and know that you can. You must visualize.

Visualization is something I have written about many times. Because of it, I have manifested more love, joy and material abundance than I could have ever imagined. Let me explain how this works.

We all have experienced a time when we thought of something and,

"Bang," there it is.

Everything you see was first a thought and then it became the chair that you are sitting on, or a pencil or a table. You must visualize everything before it becomes a physical object. The architect visualizes the house before he picks up a pencil; the poet hears the song before she writes a single word.

We all have the ability to transform and make our lives better. Start taking action right now. Be patient. Things always take longer to materialize than we expect.

Remember that when transformation comes about, you have the choice to create fear, or to face the challenge with courage and faith. The only way miracles will enter your life is if you allow them in and believe that they are in your life.

I believe in you and I know that you can have whatever you want in life. Have faith in yourself. Faith is a gift, a gift that is a great power. It is a power that can transform our lives.

 Steven E

Author Index
Introduction

We sincerely hope you have enjoyed *Wake Up… Live the Life You Love's Stories of Transformation.*

If you would like to know more about the authors or if you would like to contact one or more of them, this alphabetical index is provided for your convenience. The authors have provided contact information for your use, so feel free to take advantage of this opportunity to learn more about the authors and their ideas.

Author Index

David Alden has been teaching people how to live their dreams for over 18 years. He is also a Natural Healer and Massage Therapist and offers workshops on Inner Transformation and growth. David's passion for helping others extends from his belief that when we come from a place of unconditional love, all of our decisions lead us to the ideal path. The challenge for many people is to truly get to this place in their heart where they can be "in love" with all of life. David's passion is sharing these secrets with others, so that they may experience true joy, bliss, excitement and prosperity. David resides both in Ottawa, Ontario Canada and Brookline, Massachusetts, USA.

Phone: 613-830-1677
Email: crystaldophinangels@mac.com

AmyLee is the last Medicine Woman in her Lineage. Born to Haudenesaunee (Iroquois) parents, "She-who-Catches-the-Rainbows" continues her Elders' legacy by sharing their Storytelling Medicine, Native American Herbal Education and Products, Private Intuitive Consultations, Women's Courses, Lectures, her "Fire-Paintings" and "SongPods" and the ongoing Rehabilitation of Injured Wildlife at her Nature Sanctuary established in 1980.

Address: c/o TALON, Inc. 3225 S. McLeod, Suite 100, LV, NV 89121
Telephone: 1-888-ASK-ESSA
Websites: www.HerNativeRoots.com; www.MedWom.com
Email: Answers@HerNativeRoots.com; Talon@Tusco.net

Lee is a former television producer and business developer. He lives in Arkansas when not traveling as the co-creator of the Wake Up...Live the Life You Love book series. Lee is an author featured in more than a dozen motivational and inspirational volumes. He concentrates on bringing the power of the Wake Up network to bear on the challenges of business development. You may contact Lee at: lee@wakeuplive.com.

Michael Bennett is Professor Emeritus of Rhetoric at the University of Minnesota where he has taught for over 20 years. His award-winning teaching and research have earned him various awards. His first program for Learning Strategies Corporation, *Four Powers For Greatness: Listening, Reading, Speaking, Writing*, has been acclaimed as the most complete and concise program on the subject. Other programs and publications by Dr. Bennett include *Million Dollar Vocabulary, Efficient Reading for Managers, How to Build a Power Vocabulary,* and *Four Powers of Communication.*

Address: 9080 75th Street S., Cottage Grove, MN 55016
Phone: 651-458-0203
Website: www.LearningStrategies.com/Bennett.asp

Stories Of Transformation

Acey is a self-development enthusiast with over 22 years of business experience, he brings his unique insight to other small business owners through his website. If you have a small Business or are interested in business visit his website for a variety of business topics you can put to use today.

Website: www.atouchofbusiness.com

Constance is a certified Life/Health coach, a certified medical intuitive, and certified Four Agreements coach. She also holds workshops, gives lectures and works for various corporations coaching their employees to better health and productivity. It is her mission to share her knowledge in order to help people transform their lives and their health and thus become their highest vision of themselves.

Address: Pueblo, Colorado
Phone: 719-647-5812
Email: wisewoman42@msn.com

Taka is highly regarded as one of the best internet marketing consultants, speaker and a coach to admired entrepreneurs and companies in Japan. More than 120,000 people have studied his materials on marketing and success principles. He is also the author of four best-selling books in Japan.

Website: http://www.takaiwamoto.com
Email: taka@rocknoble.com

Shane James helps thousands of people move towards their ideal goal weight. His popular pod cast *Weight Loss and the Mind*, is heard weekly in over 20 countries by more than 100,000 people. Shane James offers live seminars and online weight loss programs at his free membership site, weightlossandthemind.com.

Websites: www.freeweightlosspodcast.com and www.weightlossandthemind.com
Email: shanejames45@hotmail.com

Dr. Kalnins has practiced clinical medicine for the last 20 years. She has been featured in the media and recognized as a top doctor. She is authoring a variety of material regarding health and other information and is a proponent of taking charge of your own health. She resides in New Jersey with her husband and daughter.

Address: Advanced Vision & Laser Care Center, Morristown, NJ 07960
Phone Number: 973-543-5669
Websites: www.njlasik.com or www.anothersideofmedicine.com
E-Mail: lindakalninsmd@aol.com

Elke Keil is certified in medical Hypnotherapy, Aura Star 2000 Counselor, and an advanced practitioner of Holistic Health. She is the owner of a small company, Shanti Living: Holistic Solutions for the Body, Mind and Spirit, in Costa Mesa, California and is studying for her PhD in hypnotherapy. She's the mother of an amazing, wonderful daughter and is a new grandmother.

Phone: 714-966-1742
Website: www.elkekeil.lifesuccessconsultants.com
Email: elkekeil@sbcglobal.net

Nami is the president of Proa, Ltd., a company that offers transformational programs and consultation/coaching to individuals and organizations. She is also the president of Proa Education, a non-profit organization that offers programs to parents and rehabilitation education to truants. Programs she offers come from her background as a physician and her English-Japanese bilingual and bicultural transformational experiences.

Address: 910-1-28-1 Ooi, Shinagawa, Tokyo 140-0014, Japan
Phone and Fax: +81 3-37746331
Website: http://www.proa.jp
Email: namik@proa.jp

Roxey Lau is a psychospiritual trailblazer, visionary, coach and mentor. Her particular brand of coaching aims to support people to create their own distinction, to do their own thing, and to define success in a manner that is deeply personal, authentic, and that resonates with their highest vision of self.

Company: Creating Personal Wealth
Address: Knoebelstr. 4b, 80538 Muenchen, Germany
Website: www.roxeylau.com
Email: info@roxeylau.com

Chunyi Lin is a certified International Qigong Master and the creator of Spring Forest Qigong. He is also a Tai Chi Master and highly skilled in Chinese herbal medicine and acupuncture. He served as Director of Qigong Programs at Anoka-Ramsey Community College in Anoka, Minnesota, from 1999 to 2004, and created the curricula for and currently services as Program Director and Lead Instructor of a fully accredited program in Spring Forest Qigong at Normandale Community College of Bloomington, Minnesota.

Address: 7520 Market Place Dr., Eden Prarie, Minnesota, 55344
Phone: 925-593-5555
Website: www.LearningStrategies.com/MasterLin.asp

Coral Majoor is a natural healer who has pursued Natural Therapy for years, including massage, chiropractic, acupuncture, and rebirthing. She is also certified in Reiki and Bowen Techniques.

Address: PO Box 233, Nerang, Gold Coast, Queensland, Australia 4211
Websites: www.majoor.mionegroup.com, www.coralmajoor.com.au
and www.maxgxl.com/globalmaxbodyfuel
E-mail: support@coralmajoor.com.au

Donald Mills has an internet business dedicated to helping people find ways to supplement their income and live in financial independence. Don and his wife, Diane, live in Chesapeake with their three children, Julie, Jonathan, and Jennifer.

Website: www.dwmresearch.com
E-mail: dmntprof@yahoo.com

Shirley Orf teaches Enneagram 101 based on her theory that your birth date is part of the hidden key to knowing your personality type. Do regular Numerology, then subtract one to reveal your Enneagram type which reveals your subconscious motivations. This is the basis for her next book.

Website: www.enneagrambirthdate.com
Email: enneagrambirthdate@yahoo.com

Nina Potter lives in St. Paul, Minnesota where she works and plays at her first love: raising consciousness. As a Coach and Master Hypnotist, she especially enjoys assisting clients in their discovery of the joy and peace of "Loving Your Life Now." Nina specializes in helping people to stop smoking and lose weight as an example of how all changes can make big differences in our lives.

Address: 2012 Mesabi Ave., Maplewood, MN 55109
Phone: 888-978-9118
Website: www.NinaPotterCoach.com

The Anthony Robbins Foundation is a non-profit organization created to empower individuals and organizations to make a significant difference in the quality of life for people who are often forgotten—youth, homeless and hungry, prisoners, elderly and disabled. Our international coalition of caring volunteers provides the vision, the inspiration, the finest resources and the specific strategies needed to empower these important members of our society.

Phone: 1-800-554-0619 or 1-858-535-6295
Website: www.anthonyrobbinsfoundation.org
E-mail: foundation@anthonyrobbinsfoundation.org

Marilyn is a strategist, author, and speaker. Her diverse and multi-faceted career path has encompassed education, sales, marketing, management, and work with corporations. Her university degrees include a Doctorate in Leadership.

Website: www.DrMarilyn.biz
Email: DrMarilyn@MRFGlobal.biz

Dr. Maxwell Synsvoll is a graduate of Northwestern College of Chiropractic. He holds degrees in chiropractic and human biology. He has completed continuing education with the International Pediatric Chiropractic Association and the Gonstead Seminar of Chiropractic. In addition to hosting workplace safety seminars and teaching people about the causes and prevention of disease, Dr. Maxwell is a father, son, brother, uncle and husband to his wife Candis, who is a physical therapist.

Company: Battle Ground Chiropractic
Telephone: 360-687-6307
Email: synsvollchiro@aol.com

Brian is the most listened to audio author on personal and business success in the world today. His fast-moving talks and seminars on leadership, sales, managerial effectiveness and business strategy are loaded with powerful, proven ideas and strategies that people can immediately apply to get better results in every area.

Company: Brian Tracy International
Address: 462 Stevens Ave., Suite 202, Solana Beach, CA 92075
Phone: 858-481-2977
Website: www.briantracy.com
E-mail: mschiller@briantracy.com

Sensei Tristan is the founder of the Austin Martial Arts Academy and has been practicing and teaching martial arts and self-defense for the past 25 years. Additionally he is the co-owner of All Ways Zen, an online wellness and mind-body fitness company. After recovering from a serious back injury that lasted five years Sensei Tristan created DVD programs for healing and strengthening the mind and body. These courses include Martial Yoga, Zen Nature Qigong, The Art of Mushin, Mind-Body Magic and Neigong: Self Mastery Skills. Sensei Tristan loves helping people evolve physically, mentally, emotionally and spiritually.

Websites: www.allwayszen.com or www.austinmartialarts.com

A. Alex Viefhaus is an Australian PhotoReading Instructor for Learning Strategies Corporation and a Coach. Her training room is on the campus of the University of Western Sydney Blacktown Campus at Quakers Hill, where she holds regular monthly PhotoReading classes. She will soon expand her teaching to other states. Being an expert PhotoReader leaves her with plenty of free time to travel and to be a writer, photographer, artist, and mentor to her friends.

Address: P.O. Box 6638, Blacktown NSW 2148, Australia
Phone: +61 2-98533266
Website: www.PhotoReading.com.au

Kris Zimmermann owns and runs Healing Energies Inc., helping the world to heal by helping people, animals and environments.

Address: P.O. Box 3464, Bozeman, MT 59772
Phone: 406-587-6351
Websites: www.kriszimmermann.com or www.healingenergiesinc.com
Email: kz@kriszimmermann.com

Learning Strategies Corporation
Maximize your full potential

Founded in 1981 as a consulting and training company, Learning Strategies Corporation has evolved into a premier provider of self-improvement, education, and health programs. Learning Strategies combines four dynamic mind/body/spirit technologies that individually have affected the lives of millions into a potent force to help people maximize their potential.

With founder Paul R. Scheele, Learning Strategies has focused its unique expertise in neuro-linguistic programming, accelerated learning, preconscious processing, and universal energy into a highly effective family of self-growth programs. These include: the *PhotoReading* whole mind system, a remarkable program that helps people read books at lightning speed; *Paraliminal* CDs, pleasurable audio programs that stimulate the mind in ways that generate near instant results in every area of life; and the *Spring Forest Qigong* and *Diamond Feng Shui* personal learning courses, which help people influence the energy within themselves and in their environment to support their own successes, relationships, health, and spiritual growth.

Learning Strategies offers a number of other innovative programs with an unmatched blend of experiential process, insightful instruction, and success coaching. Clients see progress from the first day on their way to living a life of greater abundance and well-being. Visit www.LearningStrategies.com

For more information,
Learning Strategies Corporation
2000 Plymouth Road
Minnetonka, Minnesota 55305 USA

Toll-free: 1-888-800-2688
1-952-767-9800
www.LearningStrategies.com
Mail@LearningStrategies.com

NOTES AND PERSONAL REFLECTIONS

NOTES AND PERSONAL REFLECTIONS

_____
_____
_____
_____
_____
_____
_____
_____
_____
_____
_____
_____
_____
_____
_____
_____
_____
_____
_____
_____
_____
_____
_____
_____
_____